Chinese Characters

Chinese Characters

JUSTIN WINSLETT

SIRIUS

SIRIUS

This edition published in 2022 by Sirius Publishing, a division of
Arcturus Publishing Limited,
26/27 Bickels Yard, 151–153 Bermondsey Street,
London SE1 3HA

Copyright © Arcturus Holdings Limited

ISBN: 978-1-3988-2089-0
AD010707UK

Printed in China

Contents

Introduction

Chinese characters have offered mystery and wonder to people the world over for centuries. This is curious given that they are, for all intents and purposes, examples of an orthographic system that share features and practices common to all other writing systems in the world. The letters on this page share many of the same basic features, from a technical point of view, with Chinese characters and both are equally impressive innovations developed by humans to encode and transmit information.

The mystery and wonder that people have felt, and still feel, can often be attributed to social, cultural and even political factors, the confusion of Chinese characters with other aspects of culture, or more often than not lack of understanding and knowledge of what they are and how they work. These issues have appeared from the very beginnings of the study of Chinese characters. The first work to offer an understanding of them, the *Shuowen jiezi* 說文解字, a text attributed to a scholar named Xu Shen 許慎 (*c*.58–148 CE), comes from almost 2,000 years ago. Not only does this work bring with it several social and cultural assumptions that would have made sense to the subjects of the Han Empire in which Xu Shen lived, but by Xu Shen's time, Chinese characters had already been evolving and in use for at least 1,000 years; their origin and purpose was already being obscured and lost to successive epochs. It is no surprise, then, that even today many people who encounter Chinese characters are both fascinated and perplexed by them, not least because of their ubiquity and strong association with China and Chinese culture.

This book will aim to shed light on what Chinese characters are, dispel the many myths and misunderstandings about them and give the reader an insight into how they work and the fascinating realities behind them. It will do this in a somewhat similar manner to how people in traditional China would have learnt their first characters, by looking at the first 208 characters of a text known as the *Qianzi wen* 千字文 (6th century CE), which was one of a number of primers that would inform the education of many people who would first set about to learn how to read and write with these characters until the 20th century.

There has been a wealth of scholarly research on Chinese characters over the past 40 years that has coincided with many archaeological discoveries and greater interest in Asian linguistics. While it is not possible to condense all of this into the pages of this book, the introduction will help highlight some of this to the reader and provide a stepping-stone into this fascinating script.

The Basics

Chinese characters, which in Chinese are referred to as *hànzì* 漢字, represent an orthography, (this refers to both the units used to write and the way those units are organized and developed) that today is primarily used to write East Asian languages – predominantly Mandarin and Cantonese, Japanese and to a lesser extent Korean. They have been used to write other languages in the past, notably Classical Chinese and Vietnamese, and they have also found use in decoration and art across the globe, particularly as globalization has led to their widespread appearance.

At their root, they are a writing system that follows many of the rules and conventions of other writing systems found around the world. Just like the letters one reads on this page, a Chinese character has a physical form, a *glyph*, that has a phonetic value that corresponds to a basic sound unit in a language, what can be called a *mora*. Many, though not all, Chinese characters have a *semantic value* as well, unlike the letters used on this page. This constitutes a third aspect to Chinese characters, which is not present in many other orthographies and has often drawn the most attention. These three aspects are what informs the basic nature of what linguistically are termed *Sinitic orthographies*.

The exact origin for these characters is not clear, albeit in their long history of use numerous myths and legends have arisen, usually attributing them to legendary cultural heroes or even deities. Although perhaps not gifted by the gods, the earliest examples of recognizable Chinese characters

are on a collection of divinatory remains collectively referred to as Oracle Bone Inscriptions whose purpose was to speak to the divine. Some of these characters gave rise to characters still in use today, and the basic principles that inform the modern orthographies derived from them are clearly present even in this early script.

Many orthographies either based on or inspired by this script would arise and develop over the next 3,000 years. These were more numerous in the past, but those that remain today are used to write some of the major languages of the world.

The main characters seen in this book are those known as 'traditional' Chinese, or *fantizi* 繁體字, one of the major orthographies used to write Mandarin and the principal way to write Classical Chinese. Alongside it, and sharing many of the same characters, are those commonly known as 'simplified Chinese', or *jiantizi* 简体字, which is primarily used to write Mandarin in the People's Republic of China and Singapore. These two sets share many characters and thus overlap to a large degree, and are often thought of as just two different versions of the same orthography.

Alongside these two sets are *kyūjitai* 舊字體 and *shinjitai* 新字体, two orthographies used to write Chinese characters used in Japanese. These two overlap greatly with *fantizi* and *jiantizi*, with most of the characters being the same amongst them, and indeed *kyūjitai* and *fantizi* are often thought of as identical.

That these different orthographies share most characters in common contributes to one of the major cornerstones of culture in East Asia. This 'shared' writing system, despite the radically different spoken languages in the region, has always been something called upon as a mark and root of common culture in the region. Although there are variations between the systems they are based on the same characters and even the same principles for the development of new characters.

Strokes

All characters can be understood to be composed of a number of 'strokes'. These strokes have, over time, developed into specific forms and as such characters, in many cases, show a regular and predictable pattern of construction.

The number of basic strokes is somewhat debated depending on the script used, but convention from at least the 14th century holds that there are eight basic strokes as exemplified by the character *yǒng* 永. While there are exceptions, for the most part characters have now been standardized with these strokes.

The technology used to write is inseparable from the evolution of writing and the graphic nature of modern Chinese characters is based primarily on the tradition of writing them with an ink brush on a fibrous medium, traditionally bamboo strips. The strokes are based on the conceit that an ink brush is generally writing the character with left to right motions starting from the top of the character and any 'outer components' before moving down and completing any 'inner components'.

Hence, characters today not only are composed of the same basic fundamental components, but these components have a predictable way in which they are organised, known as 'stroke order', which is essential to learning how to write.

These strokes and their order also inform how the characters are reduced into their cursive and short and simplified forms. Further, these principles have inspired derived orthographies such as the *kana* used in conjunction with Chinese characters to write modern Japanese, where the *kana* are directly derived characters, stylized upon calligraphic adaptations from their stroke order.

Components and Radicals

Although characters are made up of similar strokes, the usual approach is to think of characters as being composed of a set number of regular components, referred to as 'radicals' in English, *bùshǒu* 部首 in Mandarin. This is first attested by the *Shuowen jiezi* (*c*.121 CE) which not only conceives characters as being made up of a discrete and regular set of components but organizes and indexes them based on a fundamental set of these components.

These radicals are thought of, and in some cases are, individual characters in their own right, and it is their combination with each other that produces the majority of characters that one uses to write. The idea that characters are built up of components informs not only how people think of characters but how they are indexed in dictionaries, indices and other reference works. It is not uncommon to describe how to write a character with the radicals and components that compose it and there are even riddles, puns and other forms of word play that make use of these radicals.

The radicals and components, however, are somewhat arbitrary and do not entirely represent all characters present, and indeed over the course of time some characters have been modified by the addition of or changing of radicals to regularize and rationalize them. Further, some components are added to characters where they were already present but either had been rendered unrecognizable by the many regularizations of the script, or because writers felt this would make the meaning clearer, a linguistic process called *hypercorrection*.

The number of radicals has varied over time. However, it is convention today to use the 214 radical system proposed by the *Kangxi zidian* 康熙字典 (1716), or variants of it.

The Six Writings

The *Shuowen jiezi* argues that the characters in use during the Han could be understood as fitting into six categories, what it terms the 'Six Writings' 六書. Although these six categories do not take into account how many of the characters are actually composed, they do represent one of the earliest known attempts to understand how the characters of the time functioned and gave rise to useful insights into their development. Further, these Six Writings have served as guiding principles for character development since the Han dynasty.

The *Shuowen jiezi* argues that characters can be understood as:

Pictograms 象形字

A small minority of characters can be understood as graphical representations of their semantic meaning. These constitute a very small minority of characters, though they also serve as the basis for the radical system proposed by the *Shuowen jiezi*, and hence are important components for other characters.

Indicative Characters 指事字

These characters can be understood as *intuitive* graphical representations of their semantic meaning, in some cases through slight modification of characters classified as pictograms. How these are different from characters in other categories, particularly pictograms, is not entirely clear.

Compound Ideographs 會議字

Characters in this class are thought to be made up of two or more basic characters whose combination yields their semantic meaning. A classic example is the character 'bright' *míng* 明 which can be understood as being the 'pictogram' characters 'sun' *rì* 日 and 'moon' *yuè* 月 combined. More recent work particularly on Old Chinese has thrown this category into question, arguing that in many cases what the *Shuowen jiezi* argues to be 'compound ideographs' should be understood as 'phono-semantic compounds'.

Rebus Characters 假借字

Characters in this class are 'borrowed', meaning their phonetic value is being used to represent a word with a different meaning from the initial character because the two words are homophones. These characters are not comprehensible on any 'graphical' level. An example would be the character *zhī* 之, which has a number of meanings in Classical Chinese, and to a lesser extent in modern varieties, as either a particle that creates a noun phrase, a third person object pronoun or a verb meaning 'to go'. The *Shuowen jiezi* argues that it initially meant 'to grow' to explain its graphic component, while its other meanings merely use the character since they are homophonous or near homophonous with the word 'to go'. Although some of these arguments are considered dubious, the use of characters for purely phonetic purposes is incredibly frequent across the long history of their use, and speaks to the strong phonetic aspect of Sinitic orthography.

Phono-semantic compounds 形聲字

By far the largest category, characters of this class are meant to be composed of at least two components, often understood as characters in their own right, with at least one of the components suggesting the semantic aspect of the character and the other representing the phonetic aspect. The characters 'river' *hé* 河, 'lake' *hú* 湖, and 'sea' *hái* 海, all share the same component on the left which is understood to be a reduced form of the 'pictogram' for 'water' *shuǐ* 水, which provides insight into the semantic meaning of each character, which do indeed all refer to bodies of water. The component on the right, respectively *kě* 可, *hú* 胡, and *měi* 每, are meant to suggest the phonetic component. As can be seen, though, this phonetic component is not entirely 'reliable' in providing an accurate pronunciation for the character. The first example only yields a near homophone while the third example offers two different sounds. Some of this can be explained by the differences in the pronunciation of earlier forms of Sinitic languages, particularly as many of these characters were developed prior to the existence of modern Mandarin. In other instances, the difference may be intentional.

Mutually Explanatory Characters 轉注字

A number of characters are thought to be mutually related and thus their meanings explain each other. The primary example are the characters 'to examine' *kǎo* 考 and 'old' *lǎo* 老, as inverted forms of each other. This category was considered highly dubious even by early scholars, and it is also the least explained or well understood. Its presence speaks to the *Shuowen jiezi*'s own intellectual agenda. More recent insight into Old Chinese reconstruction suggests that these two words may have been homophones, which suggests an as-of-yet poorly understood connection between words that the compilers of the *Shuowen jiezi* may have been privy to.

Myths

Characters are words.
It is important to understand that characters and words are not necessarily the same thing. Although many characters do have a semantic value that represents a word, this is not always the case and there is rarely a one-to-one correlation. Many are just used for their phonetic value or represent grammatical particles, which though often thought of as a type of word, function very differently. Likewise, many words require multiple characters to write, as these words have multiple mora, akin to polysyllabic words in English, and as the basic principle of characters is to only represent single mora, they must be bound with other characters to make meaningful words. Indeed, the number of words in Chinese and Japanese today far surpass the number of characters that are in general use.

Characters are pictures.
Although there are some characters that are pictograms, the vast majority in use are not and do not in any way help to 'paint a picture' of what the character is referring to.

Characters tell stories.
Though there are a few characters whose components all offer semantic values which together 'suggest' what the meaning of the character may be, these are rare and often do not provide a detailed story, let alone how the character came to be. Some of the suggestions seem somewhat oblique and require a degree of imagination. Although learners of these characters are often told the 'story' that explains the character by their teachings, more often than not, these stories are what are understood in linguistics as *folk etymologies*. Folk etymologies are explanations of the origin of linguistic concepts, often in English the origin of words, that though commonly held are not actually supported by etymological study.

Characters can be used to write any language.

While it is possible to adapt orthographies to any language, it is rarely done simply by writing in another script. Rather, as orthographies are strongly influenced by the languages that use them, they are adapted to best serve the expectations of the communities employing them. For much of its history, Sinitic scripts have been used predominantly by Sinitic languages which have certain phonetic principles and grammatical similarities – the most important of which include morae made up of an initial and final sound, and in some cases a tone, and being what are known as 'isolating' languages, where there is a one-to-one relationship between the number of sounds to a word, roughly meaning words do not inflect or conjugate. When adapted to languages that differ, such as Japanese, Korean and Vietnamese, various strategies have been employed, from the development of the derived orthographies of *hiragana* and *katakana* to supplement characters and reflect Japanese agglutinating grammar to the Vietnamese development of *chunom* to reflect Vietnamese vocabulary and grammatical particles.

Interestingly, reconstruction of Old Chinese suggests that it was not an 'isolating' language like modern forms of Chinese, and instead had a number of affixes, sounds attached to the word, to indicate syntactic or lexical change. This has vestigial traces in a number of Chinese characters and words, and will be seen in some of the Characters in this book where certain components of characters are added to mark this addition of an affix. Unlike the very formal systems that evolved in Japanese, however, the traces seem somewhat random and are not regular suggesting that the system did not develop very far, particularly as these affixes are clearly lost by Middle Chinese, suggesting they may have been disappearing by the time that writing became more widespread.

Traditional Characters are Classical and Simplified are Mandarin.

Fantizi characters are sometimes translated into English as 'traditional' whilst *jiantizi* are sometimes called 'simplified'. This may have contributed to the misunderstanding that *fantizi* are Classical Chinese, archaic, or obsolete.

However, these two character sets are actually just two different ways to write both Mandarin and Classical Chinese, and differences in use are usually political or cultural. Indeed, most characters are the same between them, and the 'simplified' characters are often less complex iterations of the characters that have existed for centuries. Some scholars prefer to translate *fantizi* as 'full form' to avoid this confusion.

The *Qianzi wen*

The characters that follow are taken from the text called the *Qianzi wen* 千字文, also known in English as the *Thousand Character Classic*. As the name suggests, this text is composed of a thousand characters organized into a poem that serves as a primer to learn how to read and write characters as well as to understand basic words and concepts that inform many texts written in Classical Chinese. The text's origins are not entirely clear. A number of tales attributed the text's existence to Emperor Wu of the Liang Empire (502–557 CE), a noted historical personage, but who he commissioned to compose it and to what end often varies. Numerous copies have been uncovered in excavations at Dunhuang in western China, where many of this city's book depositories would have been sealed in the Tang dynasty (618–907). This suggests that its use as a primer was already well established in the first millennium CE given Dunhuang's role as a centre for learning and study at that time.

By the late imperial period, when the civil service exam produced not only an education system but also an entire economy around learning to pass the exam, this text became an indispensable primer for learning how to read and write. It would be used alongside two other texts, the *Sanzijing* 三字經 and the *Baijiaxing* 百家姓, as the introduction to reading and writing for individuals before they began on the core texts that made up the canon of the civil service exam. These texts, then, formed the bedrock of the education of the literati who would not only be expected to be familiar with them, but recite them from memory. Such primers would also have been key to the education of children of merchants, aristocrats and other learners across East Asia too.

While reading through the first 208 characters of this text, the characters will be presented and explained for their meaning, understanding of etymology, and some additional words. This exposure would not be unlike what young scholars of Classical Chinese would be required to learn, albeit without the repetition of writing, rote learning of the texts, and drilling of characters.

Conventions

In the following pages, each character appears in its traditional (*fantizi*) form first, followed by the simplified (*jiantizi*) iteration below if present. If the *shinjitai* iteration differs from either the traditional or the simplified, then it will be placed below the simplified. In the lower right will be displayed the modern Mandarin pronunciation, followed by the Middle Chinese and then concluding with the Old Chinese. A description of its basic meaning, how the character is composed, and how it is used in the *Qianzi wen*, if different from its basic meaning, then follows.

The forms presented in this book represent the 'standard' glyphs that one is most likely to see in current use as many of the other iterations are either niche to specific communities, obsolete or simply academic curiosities.

The phonetic sounds (or 'glosses') are provided to understand how the characters have developed. Modern Mandarin glosses are provided in standard pinyin. The Middle Chinese provided reflects a close approximation of the main form of Sinitic languages from roughly the first millennium CE primarily based on the *Qieyun* 切韻, a dictionary dated to 601 CE and subsequent dictionaries based off of it that recorded phonetic information at the time. The Old Chinese, which effectively shows what may have been some of the basic sounds during the first millennium BCE has been 'reconstructed' from a variety of sources. Both Middle Chinese and Old Chinese are given in their conventional reconstructions, which may look somewhat alien, but they are written in this way so that other paleolinguists can understand the phonetic features of their reconstruction.

Characters of the Qianzi wen

tiān

tʰien

*thîn

Sky

At its basic level, this character can refer to the sky and through extension heaven, a connection seen in many languages across the world. In early Chinese texts, Heaven is represented in a diverse number of ways from amorphous force to anthropomorphic deity. It is also spoken of as a locale inhabited by extrahumans, often literally in the territory of the sky. The glyph seen here is often explained as being a line placed above the character for *dà* 大, which usually means 'to be big'. However, earlier forms of the glyph suggest other graphical connections particularly to glyphs with the meanings of rulers, deities and evening lightning.

In the context of the *Qianzi wen*, this character is bound to the next character *dí* 地 to mean 'the world'.

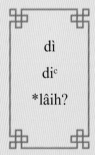

dì

dⁱᶜ

*lâih?

Earth

This character means earth in English, with extended meanings of place or location.

It is graphically composed of two other components – the glyph on the left, the character *tǔ* 土, also means earth, though with extended meanings of soil or ground, and the glyph on the right, the character *yě* 也, is a linguistic particle with a number of syntactic functions depending on which form of Sinitic one is using. This in theory suggests the phonetic element of the character, and illustrates the divergence in modern Mandarin, as the sound of *yě* is not close to *dì*. Their sounds in Old Chinese, however, were likely much closer, as the Old Chinese reconstruction was something akin to *lâih?, which is much closer to the Old Chinese reconstruction for *yě* – *laʔ ?.

In the context of the Qianzi wen, this character is bound in a word with the prior character for heaven, meaning 'the world'.

xuán

ɣiwen

*wîn

Darkness

This character means to be dark, dim or can refer to darkness and by extension the mysterious or unknown.

There is little in the graphical value of the glyph to suggest either its semantic or phonetic value, and its components do not stand for characters in their own right. This could suggest that earlier forms of the glyph have been standardized to the point that any intentional construction has been lost. It could also have been borrowed, owing to phonetic similarity in early forms of the language.

In the context of the *Qianzi wen*, this character is bound with the next character to create a somewhat esoteric word that is understood to describe the appearance of both heaven and earth.

SIMPLIFIED

huáng

ɣuâŋ

*wâŋ

Yellow

This character means yellow, brown, ochre.

The character itself is ambiguous as to its construction, with nothing suggesting its semantic or phonetic meaning. Its components represent the regularizations that have led to the way modern characters look. However, early on it was considered one of the basic radicals, and as such has generally been understood as a component of other characters rather than made up of components in its own right.

As this colour has many common metaphorical relationships and major cultural significance, it is often found in compounds or as a modifier suggesting other concepts. For instance, it has a strong association as the 'imperial colour'.

In the context of the *Qianzi wen*, it is bound with the character before it to create a word that suggests the appearance of the heaven and earth.

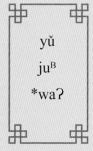

yǔ
juᴮ
*waʔ

Space

This character's earliest meanings are somewhat obscure. Its appearance in texts from the earliest strata of written Chinese has led to several commentators through the ages to suggest its semantic value, as the eaves of a building or a domicile itself. These context-dependent meanings are compounded by the rarity of its use on its own in later texts, often found bound to the following character *zhòu* 宙.

The character is made up of two components, with the topmost suggesting semantic meaning. Although not employed as a character in its own right, this component often suggests meanings related to buildings, houses or other domiciles. The bottom component is a character read as *yú* and serves as a clear phonetic.

In the context of the *Qianzi wen*, this character is bound to the following character to make a word that in modern Mandarin is understood to mean the universe. However, in earlier contexts it could also be understood as the world.

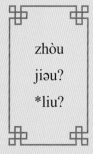

zhòu
jiəuʔ
*liuʔ

Time

This character's use on its own is somewhat sparing, as it is often bound with *yǔ* 宇. When it appears on its own, it relates to the expanse of time.

The top component is the radical associated with buildings, houses or domiciles, while the bottom component, *yóu* 由, suggests its phonetic rendering, though in modern Mandarin, *yóu* and *zhòu* are rhymes rather than homophones. That these characters share similar constructions supports the idea that they exist as a bound pair.

In the context of the *Qianzi wen*, this character is bound with the one before it to mean the world in its entirety.

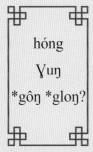

hóng

ɣuŋ

*gôŋ *gloŋ?

Flood

This character has two oft-cited meanings; one meaning would be a flood and the other would be to be big or grand. These meanings are often seen in earlier texts and not frequent on their own in modern Mandarin. However, due to the importance of these texts, they are often cited and terms from them frequently employed, and thus the character is often seen in a number of bound forms.

The composition has the radical for water on the left, oft used to suggest its primary meaning was originally a flood, and a phonetic radical on the right. This radical today would be read as *gōng*, thus yielding a rhyme rather than a homophone.

In the context of the *Qianzi wen*, this character is bound with the one that follows it, and this resultant word would refer to chaos or a primordial state.

huāng

xuâŋ

*hmâŋ

Wilderness

This character means the wilds or wilderness. By extension, it can also mean desolation, disorder and sometimes a famine or other catastrophe.

Upon first glance, the character would appear to follow phono-semantic principles. The top radical is an abbreviated glyph for *cǎo* 草, meaning grass and thus suggesting flora. The radical below suggests the sound, which is also meant to be *huāng*. However, the bottom radical is itself made up of distinct units, both of which can be characters in their own right. That the character *huāng* is found without the top radical in the same capacity in early texts would suggest that the addition of the top radical may be a 'hypercorrection' to make the glyph follow phono-semantic principles.

In the context of the *Qianzi wen*, this character is bound with the one before it to mean chaos or a primordial state.

rì

ńźjet

*nit

Sun

This character means the sun, and by extrapolation, owing to the movement of the sun across the sky and then its absence at night, the day.

One of the most basic and earliest attested glyphs, this character is one of the few that can actually be argued to be a pictogram with its modern, stylized form, meant to simply be the image of the sun.

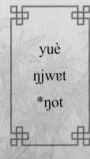

yuè

ŋjwɐt

*ŋot

Moon

This character means the moon, and by extrapolation, due to the observation of the cycle of the moon in the sky from the surface of the Earth, a month.

Like *rì*, this character is also a pictogram, and it appears in early forms of Sinitic as far back as oracle bones, with graphic stylization being the most marked example of change in various forms of Sinitic writing.

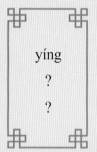

yíng

?

?

Full

This character means simply to be full.

The bottom radical means a plate or bowl, and thus is a semantic component, obliquely suggesting something that could be full. The top radical indicates an earlier variant form of another character *yíng* 贏, which would suggest the pronunciation.

In the context of the *Qianzi wen*, the character exists in a bound form with the following character to mean something like 'to cycle through the sky', in reference to the sun and moon before them.

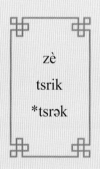

zè

tsrik

*tsrək

Meridian

A rarely seen character on its own, this character indicates the meridian and by extension the afternoon.

The top component should be recognizable as the character for sun. The bottom component is read as *zè* as well, which would provide the phonetic. Though rarely seen, it has the meaning 'to tilt', and so may also provide semantic value owing to the tilted rotation of the sun in the sky as perceived in temperate latitudes.

In the context of the *Qianzi wen*, the character here exists in a bound form with the character before it to mean something akin to 'to cycle through the sky' in reference to the sun and moon before them.

chén

źjen

*dən

Stars

This character means stars. As the word is a collective, it doesn't refer to a star on its own. It can suggest through extrapolation all celestial bodies, including the sun and moon. It is also the name of one of the Terrestrial Branches *dìzhī* 地支, which are a sequence of twelve that see a multitude of uses. The fifth in the sequence, it sees constant use in time keeping, along with another sequence of ten the Celestial Stems *tiāngān* 天干, to name things such as the hours or years.

The glyph is a radical serving to index the other characters, although it can be further subdivided.

In the context of the *Qianzi wen*, it is in a bound compound with the preceding character referring to the constellations.

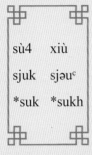

sù4	xiù
sjuk	sjəu^c
*suk	*sukh

Constellation

The character here is often read as *sù* wherein it means to lodge or a lodging. However, it has a second reading, that of *xiù*, in which it refers to constellations.

The top radical refers to buildings, houses or domiciles, something in keeping with its reading as *sù*. The bottom component, however, would be read as *bài* 佰. Its old and middle Chinese pronunciations do not match, which would indicate this component is not meant to serve as a phonetic gloss. Likewise, it is made up of two components, which has given rise to the belief that the right radical, person, and the left component, one hundred, indicate people and wealth 'stored' beneath the 'roof'. This may be etymologically dubious, though it does serve as an interesting pneumonic to remember the components of the character.

In the context of the *Qianzi wen*, the character is bound to the character before it to create a word meaning constellation. Owing to this, in Mandarin it is preferred to be read as *xiù*.

liè

ljät

*rat

Order/row

This character means to order or array as a verb and as a noun means row or list.

The components of the character do not clearly suggest its meaning or pronunciation. The right unit *dǎi* 歹 means bad. It is an adjusted form of *dāo* 刀, which means blade. Regularization of former components into more contemporary forms may have rendered it ambiguous, or perhaps it was borrowed for its sound.

SIMPLIFIED

张

zhāng

tjaŋ

*traŋ

Open

This character is frequently seen today in Mandarin as a proper noun, and it is a common surname shared by many people. It is also a verb meaning to open, and by extension to appear, activate, and turn on.

The left radical is a pictogram of a bow, which perhaps obliquely suggests the drawing of a bow as a form of opening, while the right is read as both *cháng* and *zhāng* in Mandarin, which clearly suggests a similar reading. It is also possible that the right component was added as a means of disambiguating this character from *cháng/zhāng* 長, which is another common surname and has different but very commonly used meanings such as to grow or be senior.

hán

Ɣân

*gân

Cold

This character means to be cold, and by extension is often used as a word for winter.

It contains the building radical at the top, and unclear components beneath. Although some scholars have suggested the bottom two dots represent the abbreviated ice radical *bīng* 冰, this is somewhat of a stretch, as this form is generally seen in the left portion of the glyph and stylized with different strokes. This form may be the result of regularization into standard strokes and radicals.

SIMPLIFIED

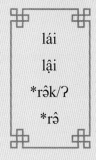

lái

lậi

*rôk/ʔ

*rô

Come

This character means to come.

The character is often used as an example of a compound ideograph, where its components suggest its meaning. In this case, it represents two people, *rén* 人, coming together under a tree, *mù* 木. None of the individual components provide a phonetic suggestion in either modern or older forms of the language. A large number of variant forms of this character are represented in earlier texts, and its current construction may be the result of regularization of components.

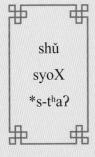

Warm

This character means to be warm, and by extension is often used as a word for summer.

The top radical is that for sun, which would suggest warmth and heat. The bottom component, *zhě* 者, is ambiguous to the phonetic value in modern Mandarin, but in Old Chinese, it is reconstructed as *ta?, which is a nearer homophone to the Old Chinese reconstruction of this character. A common, though dubious, story about this character deconstructs the bottom component further and suggests the 'sun' in it provides further semantic value.

shǔ
syoX
*s-tʰa?

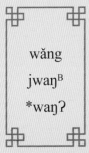

Go (towards a direction)

This character means to go, although it is more often seen in modern Mandarin as a coverb that indicates the direction towards the noun that follows it.

The left component is an abbreviated form of *xíng* 行, which also means to go, and is a semantic component of many characters involving travel. The right component, *zhǔ* 主, is likewise a radical, though it does not serve in most dictionaries to index this character. Its differing sounds also indicate it does not provide a phonetic reading, and this is also the case in earlier forms of the language. Its presence may be the result of regularization of the components of characters over the years.

wǎng
jwaŋᴮ
*waŋ?

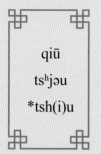

qiū

tsʰjəu

*tsh(i)u

Autumn

This character means autumn.

It, like *lái* 來, is an example of a 'compound meaning character', as neither of its very obvious components, *hé* 禾 and *huǒ* 火, suggest the phonetic value, even in earlier forms. The common explanation is that it indicates the time when grain, *hé*, turns reddish-brown, indicated by *huǒ*, which means fire and 'cooks' the grain, or relates to the usual colour of fire. This explanation is somewhat oblique, and some suggest it is again an example of the regularization of glyphs to standard forms.

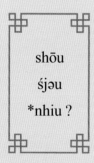

shōu

śjəu

*nhiu ?

Receive

This character represents one of the false friends between Mandarin and Classical Chinese. In Mandarin it is a verb meaning to receive; while in Classical Chinese it is a verb meaning to gather.

Both components of this character are only ever seen as components of other characters, not as characters in their own right, and both are considered by most dictionaries as radicals to index characters under. It may have had semantic or phonetic properties that have been lost owing to regularization of components, or perhaps it borrowed owing to homophones.

As the *Qianzi wen* is written in Classical Chinese, it uses the character's Classical meaning.

Winter

This character refers to the season of winter.

The top component, although a radical, is not a character in its own right, and the bottom two dots could be the ice radical, as in the character *hán* 寒.

dōng

tuoŋ

*tûŋ

Conceal

This character when read as *cáng* means to store or conceal.

The glyph can be deconstructed in a number of ways. The top component is the abbreviated form for grass, *căo* 艸. Should this be a semantic component, it could perhaps be explained by the idea of concealment in grass. The bottom component is another character in its own right, and is pronounced *cáng* or *zāng*, which also means conceal or store. The addition of the grass component may therefore be a hypercorrection.

cáng zàng

dzâŋ

*dzâŋ

SIMPLIFIED

rùn

ńźjuenᶜ

*nuns

Intercalate

This character means to intercalate as a verb or intercalary as a modifier. Although in the modern Gregorian calendar, an intercalary day is added after the 28th of February every four years to keep the calendar in sync with the movements of the sun, moon and Earth, in traditional calendars in East Asia, this was often achieved by the addition of an entire intercalary month in different years, and in some cases two would be added.

The character contains the door radical *mén* 門 as the outer component and the king radical *wáng* 王 as the inner component. As neither suggests any semantic significance or phonetic similarity, this character may have been borrowed due to homophones, or it may be the result of regularization.

In the context of the *Qianzi wen*, it is bound to the following character to mean an intercalary month.

SIMPLIFIED

yú

jiwo

*la

Surplus

This character means surplus or extra.

It combines a semantic component, the right *shì* 食, meaning to eat or food, and a phonetic component, *yú* 余, which in Classical Chinese, and some modern forms of Sinitic, is a first person pronoun and also serves as the simplified (*jiantizi*) form of the character.

In the context of the *Qianzi wen*, it is bound to the preceding character to form a word that means an intercalary month.

 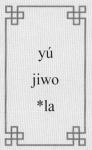

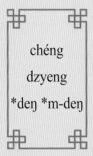

chéng

dzyeng

*deŋ *m-deŋ

Accomplish

This character means to accomplish, to complete and to become.

This character has no obvious semantic or phonetic suggestion. It is not included as a radical and instead is often indexed under *gē* 戈, a noun meaning halberd. Further, this indexing is rather unusual in that it presumes the deconstruction of a character by breaking joined strokes, something that generally runs counter to the indexing system.

SIMPLIFIED

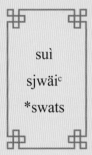

suì

sjwäi^c

*swats

Year

This character means year. In Mandarin, this character has generally been restricted to refer to year in the sense of an individual's age, though it often refers to the calendar year in Classical Chinese.

The construction of *suì* is highly ambiguous, as no component suggests an obvious phonetic or semantic element. The top component, although written today as *zhǐ* 止, to stop, is in fact an iteration of the character 屮, which has developed into a number of different iterations that mean 'to grow' amongst other things. From this, some have concluded that it has been extrapolated from the meaning of harvest.

lǜ

ljuet

*rut

Regulation

This character has the traditional meaning of regulation or stipulation, from which it derives a verbal meaning of 'to regulate' and a number of other expanded meanings related to regulation.

The character features the walk radical on the left and the glyph *yù* on the right, an archaic character that serves as a particle creating logical praxis between two clauses. The Old Chinese suggests it serves to indicate the phonetic value of the character.

In terms of the *Qianzi wen*, this character is bound to the following glyph to refer to the pipes, a specific wind instrument meant to be made of 12 bamboo pipes.

SIMPLIFIED

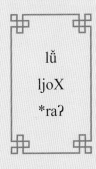

lǚ

ljoX

*ra?

Bamboo pipes (musical instrument)

This character refers to a musical instrument constructed of bamboo pipes, usually 12.

Its is composed of two mouth radicals, *kǒu* ▢ and an additional line linking them, absent in other iterations of the glyph. These may suggest the semantic value, as one must use one's mouth to play the pipes. However, it is also possible that they are actually pictographic and the regularization of the characters and their components have obscured that link.

In the context of the *Qianzi wen*, they are bound to the character before them to indicate the same musical instrument.

SIMPLIFIED

diào tiáo

dew

*dˤiw

Transfer

This character has several meanings as well as two general pronunciations in Mandarin. When said as *diào* it is a noun meaning to transfer or shift, as well as a noun referring to a tune, melody or tone. As *tiáo* it has the meaning to regulate.

It features the speech radical *yán* 言, which could serve as a semantic component. The right component, *zhōu* 周, is a proper noun, and clearly does not suggest phonetic value in Mandarin, but in Old Chinese *zhōu* would have sounded more like *tiw, which is a near homophone for *dˤiw.

In the context of the *Qianzi wen*, this character is bound to the following character to make a word that means to invigorate or revive.

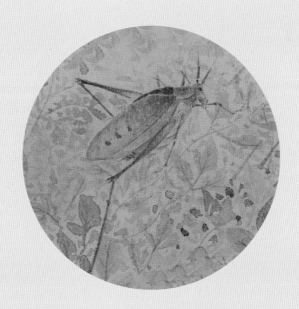

yáng

yang

*laŋ

Yang

This character's meaning is linked to another character *yín* 陰. Its meaning exists in a dichotomy with it, where what is '*yáng*' is essentially 'not *yín*'. In application, this character has a number of metaphorical meanings related to one part of other perceived binaries, such as the sun, which is identified as *yáng*, and the moon, which is identified as *yín*. This conception of binaries finds itself in many applications from epistemological categories, metaphysical concerns and even medical knowledge. As such, the character is highly context dependent.

The left component is an abbreviated form of the radical *fù* 阜, a mound or hill. If it is taken to reflect the semantic component, it may derive its meaning from the convention of referring to the sunny side of a hill as the *yáng* side and the shadowy side as the *yín* side. The right component is pronounced as *yáng* which would suggest it is the phonetic, though its meaning is identical to this character.

In the context of the *Qianzi wen*, this character is bound to the preceding character to make a word that means to invigorate or revive.

SIMPLIFIED

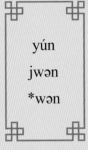

yún

jwən

*wən

Clouds

This character means clouds or a cloud.

Unlike the prior characters, its construction has both a semantic and phonetic component. The top component is the semantic one, with *yǔ* 雨, meaning rain, and is included as a radical, while the latter is *yún* 云, which on its own is a particle that indicates indirect speech or a verb meaning 'to say'.

SIMPLIFIED

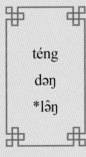

téng

dəŋ

*lə̂ŋ

Gallop

This character means to gallop, which may be metaphorically linked to its other common meaning, to soar.

The composition of this character is made up of a phonetic component, *zhèn*朕, which in Old Chinese is the near homophone *lrəmʔ, a first person pronoun used by rulers, and the semantic component, the radical *mǎ* 馬, a pictogram of a horse. Unusually, it is an example of a character with the phonetic component written first, and also one with a component of its own adjusted to accommodate the second component.

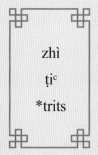

zhì

ṭiᶜ

*trits

Manifest

This character means to cause to arrive, manifest or appear.

The left component, *zhì* 至, means to arrive, suggesting semantic value. The right component is only a radical, however, not carrying any semantic or phonetic significance, and indeed it is possible to write this word with only *zhì* 至. This is because this character represents the causative form of the verb to arrive and the addition of the component actually represents the addition of an affix in Old Chinese, something lost in modern Mandarin where they are just homophones. In this case, *zhì* 至 is reconstructed as *tits with the infix 'r' in *trits representing the causative. This character is hence a vestige of Old Chinese's system of inflection.

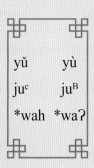

yǔ   yù

juᶜ   juᴮ

*wah   *waʔ

Rain

This character means rain or to rain, though modern Mandarin reads the noun and verb with a tonal difference – the noun being *yǔ* and the verb *yù*.

The character is a pictogram, representing a stylized form of rain falling from the sky. It is also one of the radicals with many characters, such as that for cloud, indexed under it.

Its sound difference may also indicate Old Chinese's system of affixes, in this case with a modified form indicating the verb rather than the noun, and this is attested in slight differences in both the Old and Middle Chinese.

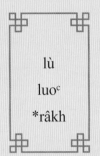

lù

luoᶜ

*rậkh

Dew

This character means dew.

The top component is that for rain, providing a semantic connection. The bottom portion provides its phonetic value, although it can be broken up further, as this character is pronounced as lù 路, meaning road.

SIMPLIFIED

结

jié

kiet

*kît

Join

This character represents the verb to knot, tie together, join or congeal. As a noun it refers to a knot or node. By extension, it is often used to indicate marriage.

The left component suggests a semantic meaning related to cloth or weaving. The *Shuowen jiezi* asserts it as a character in its own right, *mì* 糸; however, its first known attestation is in this text, suggesting that this may be a hypercorrection to create a 'character' to explain the radical. The right component is a character, *jì* 吉, which means good fortune. Though only a near homophone in modern Mandarin, in Old Chinese the reconstructions indicate they may have been near perfect homophones both, with *jì* 吉 being *kit. Given its meaning and the association of this character with marriage and the strong cultural value placed on this institution, it is a common folk etymology to argue that this provides semantic value as well.

SIMPLIFIED

wèi   wéi
jwie^c jwie
*waih *wai

Be

This character means to be, do, make or become as a verb. It is also used for a coverb, realized by being said in the fourth tone in Mandarin, to indicate that the verbal action of the sentence is being done on behalf of the noun that follows it.

This character's construction is extremely unclear and has given rise to a number of folk etymologies and scholarly arguments, and what radical to index it under varies by dictionaries given the presence of a number of possibilities. It is often suggested to be a pictogram, but the regularization of components has left it very opaque as to its antecedents.

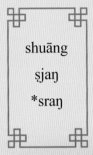

shuāng

ṣjaŋ

*sraŋ

Frost

This character means frost or rime.

The rain radical is the topmost component. The bottom provides a phonetic reading. In modern Mandarin this reads as *xiāng* 相, which can itself be broken into two other radicals. The Old Chinese offers closer phonetic readings, in this case being either *saŋh and *saŋ offered for *xiāng* 相.

Metal

This character refers to metal in a general sense. It is also used in a metonymical sense to refer specifically to gold or silver.

jīn
kjəm
*kəm

This character is also classified as one of the basic radicals in the *Shuowen jiezi* and subsequent dictionaries, and indeed serves as an indexing tool for a number of other characters. Indeed, many chemical elements discovered in modern times were coined with newly developed characters where, if they were metals, this character would be combined with another which would provide the phonetic reading, such as aluminium *lü* 鋁 or cadmium *gé* 鎘. A common folk etymology suggests it illustrates a forge, where the top portion is the roof and the bottom represents the anvil. The diagonal lines then either represent flames, the sparks from a hammer or even the people themselves working at the forge. Given the large number of explanations, this may not represent its actual derivation.

Birth

This character as a verb means to be born, give birth, create, make, produce and also to live. As a noun, it means birth, creation, production or life.

shēng
ʂɐŋ
*srêŋ

This is a pictogram, meant to represent a plant growing from the earth, although there are some that point to the upper left stroke as marking a fruit or other growth which actually represents its meaning.

lì

lieiᶜ

*rêkh *rêh

Beautiful

This character means to be beautiful.

A complex character, *lì* is a compound meaning character where both portions suggest its meaning rather than its sound. The top portion of the character, though used as the simplified (*jiantizi*) form of the character, is not seen on its own in earlier texts, and may be a pictogram of animal pelts. The bottom portion of the character, *lù* 鹿, serves as the radical the character is indexed under. The character *lù* is also a pictogram, meaning deer, although a highly regularized one. This would suggest two things that are meant to be beautiful. The Old Chinese reconstruction of the character *lù* 鹿, however, yields *rôk, which though not a perfect match, is a near homophone, suggesting that this may also serve as a phonetic gloss.

In the context of the *Qianzi wen*, this character is bound to the next one to refer to a proper noun – Lishui, a river that flows through Zhejiang province in China.

shuǐ

świᴮ

*lhui?

Water

This character, one of the most basic, means water and by extension river.

The character, in keeping with its more fundamental nature, is a pictogram. It also serves as a radical, being included in many other characters, though styled as three strokes when placed to the left of a character, such as in the character *hōng* 洪. The picture is highly stylized, however, as it is meant to be derived from the image of a stream.

In the context of the *Qianzi wen*, this character is bound to the one before it to make a proper noun – Lishui, which is a river that today flows through Zhejiang province in China.

Jade

This character means jade, and today is strongly associated with white jade.

yù

ngjowk

*ŋok

The character is an example of an 'indicative' character, where the dot in the lower right is meant to modify the overall character, which is *wáng* 王, meaning king. The base character is a stylized pictogram and the dot is meant to 'indicate' a jade talisman hanging from the king's belt. However, how this differs from a pictogram is not entirely clear, beyond it being stylized in the same manner as *wáng*.

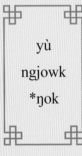

chū

tśʰjuət

*k-hlut

Emerge

This character is a verb meaning to emerge or go out.

It, like *shēng* 生, is a pictogram of a plant emerging from the ground. It differs phonetically from *shēng* and though their meanings overlap to a small degree, the two characters function differently. The similarity in their character forms may be coincidence, or may suggest that there are more than simple pictograms at play here.

SIMPLIFIED

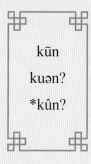

kūn

kuən?

*kûn?

[No independent meaning]

This character does not stand in place for a word and unbound is meaningless.

It follows the phono-semantic composition seen in many other characters. The top component is *shān* 山, meaning mountain, which provides semantic meaning when this character is combined with another to make a word, and it is often written without this component, while the bottom portion yields the phonetic value.

In the context of the *Qianzi wen*, this character is bound to the following one, forming Kungang, another name for the mythical Kunlun mountains, where many extrahuman and wondrous things are found.

SIMPLIFIED

gāng

mjwaŋ^B?

*maŋ??

[No independent meaning]

This character does not stand for a word and in its unbound form is meaningless.

The top portion provides the semantic meaning of mountain, something only apparent in its bound form and indeed not always included with the character. The bottom portion provides the phonetic value, which has changed in Mandarin where today it would be read as *wǎng*.

In the context of the *Qianzi wen*, this character is bound to the former character, forming Kungang, another name for the mythical Kunlun mountains, where many extrahuman and wondrous things are found.

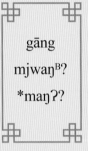

SIMPLIFIED

jiàn

kjᴇm^c

*kam

Sword

This character means sword.

This character is an example of one where the left-most, and thus first written, component does not serve as its radical for indexing or provide the semantic gloss, but rather is the phonetic component, being pronounced as *qiān* in Mandarin and *tsʰam in Old Chinese. The right component is the abbreviated form of *dāo* 刀, which means a knife or blade, providing the semantic component.

In modern use, this character is also used as an abbreviation of the University of Cambridge and things related to that university and city. In this case, it is used only for its sound value, to equate the Cam-syllable in Cambridge, with bridge being literally translated as *qiǎo* 橋.

SIMPLIFIED

háo

ɣâu

*gâu

Number

This character is a verb meaning to call or name; it can also serve as a noun meaning a name, sign or mark. In Late Imperial China, it was customary for individuals, especially among the upper and middle classes, to have multiple names which would be used in different circumstances and by different people according to a variety of social conventions. *Háo* could be thought of as aliases. In modern Mandarin it is also a noun meaning number.

The upper left component resembles *kǒu*, meaning mouth, and serves as its radical in most dictionaries. This would also suggest its semantic value, which would argue that the *hǔ* 虎 component on the right, which means tiger, may be phonetic. However, this may not be supported by Old Chinese, where *hǔ's* 虎 reconstruction would be *hlâʔ. What further complicates this glyph's origin is that the variant without the tiger component appears as early as the one with it. This would suggest the lower left component may also have some semantic value, although it is not a character on its own. A common folk etymology holds that the tiger component indicates a tiger's roar – which may be closer to its actual origin.

jù

?

?

Huge

This character means to be huge, gigantic.

It may be a pictogram of a carpenter's square, normally written as *jǔ* 矩. However, this interpretation is based on the *Shuowen jiezi*'s assertion, and lacks further attestation.

In the context of the *Qianzi wen*, this character is bound to the next one to form a proper name, which refers to the name of a mythical blade.

SIMPLIFIED

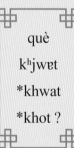

què

kʰjwɐt

*khwat

*khot ?

Lack

This character means to lack or err. As a noun it means a lack of something or an error.

The outer component is the door radical *mén* 門. This serves as a semantic component, although a rather oblique one given the word's meaning. The inner component is not a character on its own, with the left part of the inner component not being a character, although often argued to be a stylized *fǒu* 缶, and the right part is *qiān* 欠, meaning to beg, which may provide additional semantic value. The graphical similarities between this character and the two components of the inner portion of this character provide its phonetic gloss and suggest that the addition of the door radical is a hypercorrection.

In the context of the *Qianzi wen*, this character is bound to the previous one to form a proper name which refers to the name of a mythical blade.

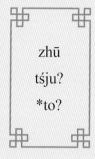

zhū
tśju?
*to?

Pearl

This character means pearl, and by extension, something precious.

The left component is an abbreviated form of the character *yú* 玉, for jade. The lack of the dot can lead to the presumption it instead refers to *wáng* 王, for king, which confusingly is also used as a radical for indexing. The right component is pronounced as *zhū* 朱 and refers to the colour crimson or vermillion.

稱

SIMPLIFIED

称

chēng
tśʰjəŋ
*thəŋ

Call

This character means to call, say or shout.

The left component is the radical *hé* for grain. The right component is a very obscure character pronounced *chèn*. Neither seems to fit the phono-semantic rules seen in other characters, although the sound difference is still very close in Mandarin. One explanation is that an older meaning of this character is to weigh, which would make sense as the semantic component for grain. Furthermore, *chèn* also has the same meaning, suggesting that this character may have its origins as a hypercorrection, which was then borrowed for the word 'to call' due to its homophonous pronunciation.

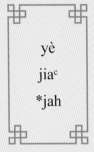

yè
jiaᶜ
*jah

Night

This character means night.

None of this character's components would suggest a phonetic reading and nothing provides an exact semantic value. Instead it is likely a compound meaning character, where it involves a person, the lower left component, asleep under a roof, the upper component, at 'night' as the bottom right component is a stylized *xī* 夕, which means evening. However, this is somewhat problematic, as this component can be understood as a number of other characters.

In the context of the *Qianzi wen*, this character is bound to the next one to form the name of a mythical pearl.

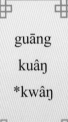

guāng
kuâŋ
*kwâŋ

Light

This character means light.

It is a pictogram depicting the rays of light from the sun either rising or setting over a landscape. The residual strokes below the middle line meant to be the 'horizon' have often raised questions as to this interpretation.

In the context of the *Qianzi wen*, this character is bound to the previous one to form the name of a mythical pearl.

果

guǒ

kuâ^B

*kôi?

Fruit

This character means fruit or nut, and by extension, result. It can also mean indeed or as expected.

It is sometimes argued that this character is a pictogram, illustrating a 'fruit' on top of a tree, *mù* 木. The way in which this fruit is stylized, however, renders it identical to *tián* 田, which means field, and may suggest fields and tree, suggesting this is not a pictogram but instead a compound meaning character.

珍

zhēn

tjen

*trən

Treasure

This character means treasure. By extension it can be used as a modifier to mean precious.

The left component is the jade radical, providing the semantic value, while the right component provides the phonetic value. However, it does not occur as a character in its own right, and may have been an earlier way of writing this character, making the addition of the jade radical a hypercorrection.

lǐ

lji^B

*rə?

Plum

This character is most often a proper noun – the common surname Li. It also has the meaning of plum and plum tree.

The top component is the character for tree, *mù* 木, and the bottom is the character for *zǐ* 子, which has a number of meanings, but at its root means child. This character is usually interpreted as a compound meaning character of a child under a tree. The thought of a child reaching for a plum may be endearing, but it could also be the case that the child refers to the plum itself.

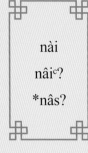

nài

nâi^c?

*nâs?

Fruit tree

This character is considered archaic and would have been considered so even when the *Qianzi wen* was written. It refers to a fruit tree, which would fit the context of this passage, usually identified as a crab apple.

Like *lǐ* 李, its top portion is the tree radical providing semantic meaning. The bottom part is read as *shī* 示 in modern Mandarin and *gih in Old Chinese, so it could not provide any phonetic value to the overall character and may be semantic as well.

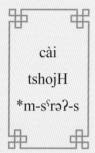

cài

tshojH

*m-sˤrəʔ-s

Plants

This character means plants, particularly vegetables and other edible plant matter. It is also used as dish or food in modern Mandarin.

The top portion of the character is the grass radical *cǎo* 艸, while the bottom is pronounced as *cǎi*, suggesting this character fits the general phono-semantic pattern seen in many characters.

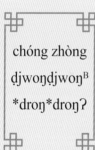

chóng zhòng

ɖjwoŋɖjwoŋ\u1d2e

*droŋ*droŋʔ

Weight

This character can mean to be heavy as a verb or weight when used as a noun. By extension it can mean something is important, weighty. It also means to duplicate. Mandarin reading rules dictate that the former is read as *zhòng*, while the latter is read as *chóng*. This may be reflective of the obsolete system of affixes in Old Chinese.

As this glyph is not easily broken into components, its construction is somewhat unclear. It could be a pictogram of boxes on a scale or an altered form of other characters. Its symmetry supports its reading as 'to duplicate', but this is a somewhat tentative explanation.

Mustard

This character means mustard, both as the plant, seed and condiment. It is often used to refer to small or trifling things.

The top portion, the grass radical *cǎo* 艸, is the semantic component. The bottom portion is another character read as *jié* in modern Mandarin.

jiè

kǎi^c

*krêts *krâts

Ginger

This character means ginger.

This character looks as if it fits the phono-semantic compound model. The top component is the grass radical *cǎo* 艸. The bottom component, while featuring in a number of characters with similar readings, is not observed on its own. It is possible that without the grass radical, it still would have meant ginger, suggesting the addition of the grass radical is a hypercorrection.

SIMPLIFIED

jiāng

kjaŋ

*kaŋ

hǎi
xậiᴮ
*hmâ?

Sea

This character means sea.

The component on the right is a stylized abbreviation of the character for water, *shuǐ* 水. This is both a radical and serves as the semantic component. On the right is the character *měi* 每, which although is not a close phoneme in modern Mandarin, was more homophonous in earlier forms of Chinese where the Old Chinese reconstruction would have been something akin to *mâ?.

SIMPLIFIED

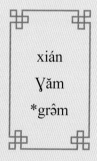

xián
Ɣăm
*grâm

Salt

This character as a noun means salt. As a verb it means to be salty.

The right side of the character serves as a phonetic component, with its modern Mandarin pronunciation being *xián*, although it is rarely used in Mandarin, as it is an adverb in Classical Chinese meaning all. The left side serves as both the semantic component and the radical, pronounced as *lǔ* on its own, and has a somewhat obscure meaning. In early texts, it seems to refer to a salt plain, though this has fallen out of use. In modern Mandarin it has gained a new lease of life, as it refers to the chemical category of elements known as halogens.

River

The character in early texts is a proper noun referring to the Yellow River. It can, however, also refer to rivers in general.

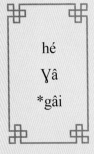

hé

ɣâ

*gâi

Its left component, and radical, is the abbreviated form of the character for water, *shuǐ* 水, which serves a semantic purpose. The right component provides the phonetic gloss – while it does not match modern Mandarin, where it would be *kě* 可, though in the Old Chinese it would be *khâiʔ.

Thin/light

This character means thin or light, and by extension to be bland or lacking in flavour. It is used here to suggest fresh in the sense of water.

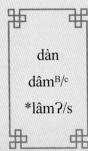

dàn

dâm[B/c]

*lâmʔ/s

The left component, the water radical, *shuǐ* 水, suggests its semantic value. The right component is today read as *yán* though in Old Chinese the sounds were more homophonous with it being closer to *lam.

SIMPLIFIED

lín

ljen

*rin

Scales

This character means scales or scutes.

The left portion of the character is *yù* 魚. It serves as both the semantic component, as it means fish, of which it is a highly stylized pictogram, and the radical. The right component features in many other characters with a similar pronunciation, suggesting it should be the phonetic, however its exact nature and status as a character in its own right are not clear, although it is suggested that it means phosphorus, which is normally written with an additional component – *lín* 磷.

SIMPLIFIED

qián

dzjäm

*dzam

Dive

This character means to dive, submerge and by extension to hide or conceal.

With the abbreviated water radical, *shuǐ* 水, on the left to serve as the semantic component, one would expect that the phonetic component should be the glyph on the right. In modern Mandarin this is not readily apparent, as this very obscure character has the phonetic value of *cǎn*. As Old Chinese reconstructions of this character are not yet available, we can't confirm if earlier forms were similar, although it is highly likely, as the difference in modern Mandarin still suggests some near homophony.

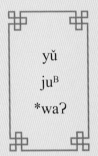

Feathers

This character means feathers. As feathers are often used as ornamentation, this character can occasionally mean ornate as well.

Although made of two components, neither serves as a phonetic or a semantic. It seems to be a pictogram of feathers, albeit a highly stylized one.

yǔ

ju[B]

*wa?

Float in the air

This character means to circle or float in the air.

The character for feathers appears on the right, which is often where the phonetic component of the character is placed, but instead here provides the semantic meaning. The character on the left should serve as the phonetic, but it is only a rhyme, *yáng*, in modern Mandarin and not a homophone.

xiáng

zjaŋ

*s-jaŋ *s-laŋ?

SIMPLIFIED

lóng

ljwoŋ

*roŋ

Dragon

This character means dragon. It is a frequently seen and oft-considered auspicious character due to its cultural significance. Given this, it has a large number of metonymical uses in many forms of Chinese.

The number of variant forms and its strong resonance as an important symbol and concept throughout the centuries have made the construction of this character the subject of much debate. None of its components provide any meaningful phonetic readings. The right component is a pictogram, meant to resemble a dragon. The lower right may be a semantic component, as the abbreviated form of *ròu* 肉, meaning meat, and thus suggests a carnivorous animal. The upper portion is the character *lì* 立, to stand or establish, though this semantic value does not fit the context of the character. These last two may be the result of the regularization of components, however.

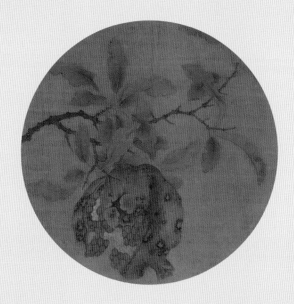

SIMPLIFIED

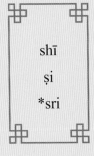

shī

sī

*sri

Teacher

This character as a noun means teacher, or more appropriately master, in the sense of a master and apprentice; or army. There is no etymological link between these two concepts – this is most likely the result of these two being homophones and thus written the same way. As a verb, this character means to take as a teacher/master.

None of this character's components are characters in their own right. Both components do resemble abbreviated forms of other characters, with the left sometimes identified as *fù* 阜, hill or mound, and the right identified as *shì* 巿, market or city. If the right component were a truncated *shì*, this would provide a phonetic component, but the Old Chinese reconstructions yield *buʔ, which is not close to this character's *sri. Further, *fù* is normally abbreviated as 阝, and why this would serve as an exception here is unclear. Again, this may be the result of the regularization of components.

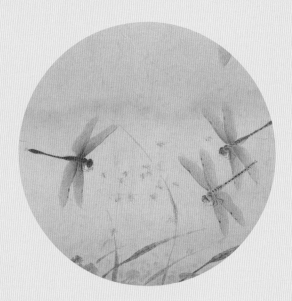

huǒ

xuâ^B

*hmâi?

Fire

This character means fire.

This character is a pictogram – a highly stylized form of flames.

In the context of the *Qianzi wen*, this character is bound to the following character as a proper noun. It refers to a culture hero and deity often mentioned in different capacities across a number of early texts – the Red Emperor 赤帝 or Yandi 炎帝.

dì

tiei^c

*têh

Emperor

This character has a number of interconnected meanings. Its earliest meaning referred to a divinity and is found in the names of a number of deities, as seen here in the *Qianzi wen*. The earliest pantheon of the Shang polity, from where the Oracle Bones emerge, seems to place Shangdi 上帝 as the highest deity. Given the strong connection between imperial authority and divinity, this character has also developed the meaning of 'emperor', meant to have been first employed in 221 BCE when the First Emperor of the Qin 秦始皇 (259–210 BCE) is meant to have combined it with the character *huáng* 皇, meaning august, to create the word for emperor – *huángdì* 皇帝.

Its construction has been subject to much analysis, with scholars variously suggesting that it is a highly stylized pictogram of a deity, a compound meaning character demonstrating a sacrifice, or perhaps draws semantic value from the character for father, *fù* 父.

SIMPLIFIED

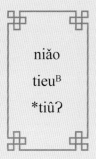

niǎo

tieu[B]

*tiû?

Bird

This character means bird. It is often confused with the very closely constructed character *wǔ* 烏, which lacks the stroke in the upper 'box' of the glyph. This is further compounded in that *wǔ* means any type of the crow family of birds.

This character is a highly stylized pictogram of a bird. This stylization becomes even more clear when compared to the character for horse, *mǎ* 馬, which shares a number of the same features, owing to the consistent regularization of strokes and components.

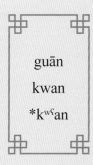

guān

kwan

*k^{wˤ}an

Official

This character means official.

This character is made up of an upper component, the 'roof' radical, which is not a character in its own right, but may provide some weak semantic significance, as well as a tool to index the character, by suggesting an official office. Indeed, a common folk etymology holds that the below component is meant to either be a pictogram of desks, officials or an official at a desk. The bottom component is not a character either, nor is it clearly abbreviated. It may be a highly stylized pictogram.

rén

ńźjen

*nin

Person

This character means person or people.

The character, one of the most basic, is a pictogram of a person standing. It can easily be confused with two other double stroke characters: *bà* 八, the number eight, which is a pictogram of the symbol for eight in counting sticks; and *rù* 入, which has the right stroke higher than the left stroke, meaning to enter.

In the context of the *Qianzi wen*, this character is bound to the next character to create a proper noun, Renhuang, a deity in a triumvirate of divinities with its counterparts being the Tianhuang 天皇 and Dihuang 地皇. These three deities, or Sanhuang 三皇, collectively serve as metonyms of a concept of rulership, that of Heaven, Earth and Man, that became more pronounced during the Tang dynasty.

huáng

ɣuâŋ

*waŋ

August

This character means to be august, and by extension means sovereign or emperor.

The bottom component is the character for king, *wáng*. With a reconstruction in Old Chinese as *waŋ, this may suggest a phonetic component to this character. However, given its meaning, it may also be the semantic component. The top component is the character *bái* 白, which means to be white. There is no metaphorical significance with this colour with regards to kingship, beyond possibly suggesting purity, and as such this character may be unusual in having a component that serves as both the phonetic and the semantic, and another that offers neither significance. The earliest iterations were pictograms depicting a ruler with an impressive crown.

In the context of the *Qianzi wen*, this character is bound to the previous character to create a proper noun, Renhuang, a deity in a triumvirate of divinities with its counterparts being the Tianhuang 天皇 and Dihuang 地皇. These three deities or Sanhuang 三皇, collectively serve as metonyms of a concept of rulership, that of Heaven, Earth and Man, that became more pronounced during the Tang dynasty.

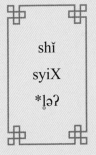

shǐ

syiX

*l̥əʔ

Start

This character means to start or begin. In Classical Chinese it is also an adverb meaning 'finally'.

The character's apparent simple construction is deceptively complex. The left component is *nǚ* 女, a character for female. It is the radical and provides indexing, leaving the semantic value somewhat suspect. The right character has two readings in modern Mandarin: *tái*, meaning platform, and *yí*, which has dubious meaning. Neither has the same phonetic value as this character in Mandarin or Old Chinese. One argument suggests that it is a compound meaning character, with *tái*, commonly written as *tāi* 胎, being the word for foetus, thus suggesting a pregnant woman and the beginning as birth.

zhì

tsyejH

*tet-s

Order

This character refers to order, structure, or control. As a noun it means system or an order.

The construction of this character is deceptively simple. The right side is the abbreviated *dāo* 刀 radical. The left is not a character in its own right, suggesting it is a highly stylized pictogram, though of what is unclear.

wén

mjuən

*mən

Writing

This character's earliest meaning was as a sign or mark. Through extension it has come to refer to writing and even literature and culture.

The character is a pictogram, though of what has been debated. Some suggest it is a tattooed individual, or stacks of writing implements or perhaps it is even more impressionistic with the lines themselves indicating a cross mark – suggesting it is one of the earliest symbols.

In the context of the *Qianzi wen*, it is bound to the following character to suggest the way and system of writing – an orthography.

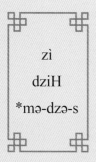

zì

dziH

*mə-dzə-s

Character (in writing)

This character means glyph, and through extension it means character.

The bottom component clearly provides a phonetic value as it is pronounced *zǐ* on its own. Why the roof radical is used for a semantic function is not entirely clear. It has been suggested that as characters and writing were the purview of officials, their association with offices explains its use. This explanation is unconvincing, and perhaps the radical was simply applied to distinguish this word from *zǐ* 子, which has other meanings.

nǎi

nậi[B]

*nə̂ʔ

Then

This character is frequently seen in Classical Chinese, but is rare in modern forms of Chinese. It is a conjunction that indicates linear praxis between clauses. This would mean it is equivalent to then in English when used in verbal sentences. In nominal sentences, a form of sentence in Classical Chinese not found in English or Mandarin, it means something more akin to actually.

The construction of this character is unknown. If it were a pictogram, it has become too stylized to be recognizable. Likewise, given its function as a particulate word, it is highly likely that it was borrowed from another word owing to sound, with the source word being unclear.

fú

bjuwk

*bək

Serve/Wear

This character as a verb means either to serve or to wear. As a noun it means clothes. These two etymologically unrelated meanings most likely rely on the same character as they have always been homophones.

The left component of the character resembles the character for moon, though the abbreviated form of *ròu* 肉, the meat radical, can be rendered in the same way. Neither provides any clear semantic value. Likewise, the right portion is ambiguous, although this is sometimes assumed to be a stylized pictogram of a hand holding something, hence providing the meaning of to serve.

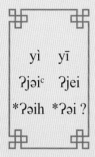

yì   yī

ʔjəiᶜ ʔjei

*ʔəih *ʔəi ?

Clothing

This character as a noun, read *yī* in Mandarin, means clothing. Specifically it referred to the coat that was worn on top of other clothing in many of the prescribed styles of dress of the various empires of the past. *Yì* is its verbal reading, meaning to wear.

The character is a pictogram of the outer coat.

In the context of the *Qianzi wen*, it is bound to the following character to mean dress or clothing in general.

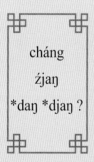

cháng

źjaŋ

*daŋ *djaŋ ?

Clothing

This character means clothing, though generally refers to the clothing worn underneath the larger coat that was custom in many of the prescribed styles of dress in past empires in China. It could refer to something akin to a petticoat or even a skirt.

The bottom part of the character is *yī*, meaning clothing. This forms the character's semantic component. The upper portion is a stylized form of the character *shàng* 尚. This is made clearer as this is the character's phonetic component, reconstructed as either *daŋh or possibly *djaŋh.

In the context of the *Qianzi wen*, the character is bound to the prior character making a word that means dress or clothing.

推

tuī

tʰuậi

*thûi

Push

This character means to push, by extension it can mean to put something forward, promote or recommend.

The left side of the character is an abbreviated form of *shǒu* 手, meaning hand. This serves as the radical and also as a semantic component. The right component is a character read as *zhuī* 隹 in modern Mandarin, providing a rhyme as the phonetic, and as *tur in Old Chinese, providing a near homophone.

位

wèi

jwiᶜ

*w(r)ə(t)s ?

Place

This character means place or location, and by extension, rank or status.

The left component is the abbreviated form of *rén* 人, person. The right component is also a character, *lì* 立, meaning to stand. The Old Chinese for this component is reconstructed as *rəp which may or may not be a near homophone owing to the tentative nature of the reconstruction of the above character. As such, it is unclear whether this is a phonetic component, or if instead it suggests meaning as well.

讓

SIMPLIFIED

让

ràng
ńźjaŋᶜ
*naŋh

Yield

This character means to yield, give way or allow.

It follows the phono-semantic construction. Its left side is the character for speech *yán* 言, providing an oblique semantic value, and while its right is pronounced as *xiāng* today, in Old Chinese it would have been something closer to *snaŋ.

SIMPLIFIED

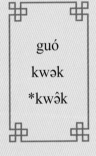

guó
kwək
*kwə̂k

Country

This character means country, polity or land. In very early texts it had a restricted meaning as the capital. The change to refer to the polity as a whole may have been brought about by a cultural convention of avoiding the names of the emperors, with the first emperor of the Han being named Bang, 邦, which also meant country, polity or land. *Guó* would have been substituted to avoid the use of the name.

The outer component provides the semantic value, indicating boundaries, something which would have made more sense with the meaning of capital, as it had defined city walls while many of the premodern empires in China did not have fixed boundaries. The inner part provides the phonetic reading, read as *huǒ* today, it would have been *wə̂k.

An oft-repeated folk etymology of this character is that the right inner portion shows a halberd, indicating defence, and the lower left strokes represent goods or valuables. This does not match with the derivation of the character, but the simplified form (*jiantizi*) of the character does align with this, substituting the character for jade as the inner component.

yǒu

jəu^B

*wə?

Have

This character means to have. It also can be used to indicate the existence construction in many forms of Chinese (i.e. there is…).

The character is a highly stylized pictogram of a hand holding meat.

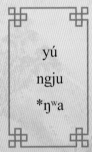

yú

ngju

*ŋ^wa

Yu

This character is a proper noun often seen today as a surname. It was also the name of an old polity in the first millennium BCE.

The bottom component serves as a phonetic gloss for the character, read as *wú* in modern Mandarin. A reconstruction in Old Chinese for this character has not been reached, so it is unclear if this is a phonetic gloss or not. The upper portion is used as the radical *hú* 虍, which some argue is a reduction of the character for tiger *hú* 虎.

In the *Qianzi wen* it refers to the clan name of a legendary ruler.

Pottery

This character means pottery or earthenware. It is also a proper noun.

táo

dâu

*lû

The left component of the character is the abbreviated form of *fù* 阜, hill or mound, which acts as both the radical and suggests the meaning. However, this somewhat oblique meaning is challenged by the right component, which, in addition to being pronounced as *táo*, also means pottery on its own. The addition of the extra component may have served some other purpose.

In the context of the *Qianzi wen*, the character is bound to the following character to create a name. In this case, it forms another name of the legendary culture hero Yao 堯, an early leader who abdicated the throne to his official Shun 舜 rather than bequeath the throne to his son.

Tang

This character is, like the characters before, a proper noun. It has been used to refer to a number of things, but perhaps most notably to the Tang dynasty (618–907 CE).

táng

dâŋ

*lâŋ

The bottom component is the mouth radical, which provides no phonetic value and it is unclear if it has any semantic importance. The top portion could be an altered *gēng* 庚, or its phonetic, but this is not seen in Mandarin or earlier forms of Chinese.

In the context of the *Qianzi wen*, this character is bound to the one before it to create the name of the legendary culture hero Yao 堯, an early leader who abdicated the throne to his official Shun 舜 rather than bequeath the throne to his son.

SIMPLIFIED

Hang

This character means to hang or to droop.

Its radical is *gōng* 弓, the character for bow. This indexing has suggested that it is a pictogram of a bow string hanging from a bow.

In the context of the *Qianzi wen*, this character is bound to the next one to make a phrase meaning to comfort the people.

diào

tek

*tʰewk

(a/the) People

This character represents the collective noun people. It contrasts with *rén* 人, which refers to a person or people in the plural sense. In very early texts, there may have been a difference between *min*, referring to the *hoi polloi*, while *rén* referred only to the aristocracy and nobility, although this distinction broke down early on.

The construction of this character is rather ambiguous. Different arguments have linked it to similar characters such as *shì* 氏, which means clan, or *mù* 母, which means mother, but these remain conjecture. Its earlier forms are equally opaque in how they relate to meaning, and it may have been borrowed owing to its phonetic similarity.

In the context of the *Qianzi wen*, the character is bound to the character before to form a verb meaning to comfort the people.

mín

mjien

*min

fá

bjwɐt

*bat

Attack

This character means to attack, cut down or fell.

It is a complex pictogram. Classified as a compound meaning character under the Six Writings system, the left component is the abbreviated form of *rén* 人, person, while the right is *gē*, meaning halberd. Neither suggests the sound, but rather it is meant to be understood as a person holding a weapon.

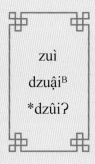

zuì

dzuậi[B]

*dzûi?

Crime

This character means wrong-doing, malfeasance or crime. It is also used to translate the concept of sin into modern Chinese.

The top portion of the character is a radical which is never seen as a character in its own right, which provides an indexing function, though how it provides a semantic value is unclear. The bottom component is the character *fēi* 非, which likewise does not provide a clear phonetic value, suggesting this may be due to the stylization of the components.

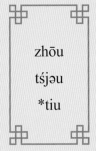

zhōu

tśjəu

*tiu

Zhou

This character is a proper noun. Its most common reference is to the Zhou dynasty (1046–256 BCE). Many early texts attribute numerous culture heroes and innovations to this period, and it was renowned as a golden age in later historiography. The character also can refer to later polities that arose in China as well as various peerages and titles. At times, the character is also used for the verb to circle as well as its derived adverb around, in all. This is sometimes written as *zhōu* 週, to disambiguate the two.

The construction would suggest that the inner part *jì* 吉, should serve as the phonetic, but as this is *kit in Old Chinese, that seems unlikely. The outer component is its radical, but as it is not a character in its own right, it is unclear what semantic value this could provide.

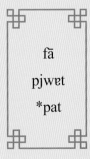

SIMPLIFIED

fā

pjwɐt

*pat

Issue

This character means to issue, emit, or send out. By extension it can also be understood as meaning to develop or open up.

A deceptively complex character, it would initially appear to follow phono-semantic principles, however the upper component is not a character in its own right but is a common radical, so though it provides indexing it does not impart any semantic value. The bottom component is not a character in its own right either, and does not impart any phonetic value. However, each sub-component does have a meaning that may provide some semantic significance. The left is *gōng* 弓, meaning bow. The right is *shū* 殳, a pictogram for a spear-like weapon. As such, it is possible that the radical component was added later to regularize the character.

殷

yīn

j+n

*ʔər

Yin

This character is a proper noun. It can generally be used as another name of the Shang dynasty 商 (1600–1046 BCE). Purists, however, argue that it only refers to the later portion of the Shang reign when they moved their capital to the city of Yin 殷, where the name emerges. The character can also represent a verb meaning to be abundant, but whether this predates the proper noun or vice versa is unclear, but would suggest phonetic borrowing in either case.

The right component, *shū* 殳, means spear and also serves as the radical. The left component is not readily identifiable. In other cases, this has suggested a highly stylized pictogram.

湯

SIMPLIFIED

汤

tāng

tʰâŋ

*lhâŋ

Soup

This character means boiled water, soup or other hot liquid. It is also a proper noun, serving as the name of the last, purportedly tyrannical, king of the Shang.

The construction follows phono-semantic principles. The left component is the water radical, *shuǐ* 水, providing a semantic clue, while the right component is *yáng* 昜.

坐

zuò

dzuâᶜ

*dzôih

Sit

This character means to sit. By extension it can also mean to occupy or hold an office.

The character is often categorized as a compound meaning character with two people 'sitting' on a mound of earth.

朝

cháo zhāo

drjew trjew

*m-taw *taw

Morning

Like many characters with two common pronunciations, this character represents two different concepts. When read as *zhāo*, this character is a time word meaning morning. When read as *cháo* this character means court as a noun. As a verb it means to attend or hold court. They share similar sounds, as near homophones, suggesting some etymological relationship between the two. Old Chinese provides further evidence, where one is clearly a modification of the other with the prefix 'm'.

The right component is the character for moon, which could provide semantic meaning. The left component is a bit more confusing, though is often understood as a variant form of the character *chuó* 卓. However, the early glyphs attested in bronze seals differ and may even suggest a pictographic component to the overall character now lost. This is further reinforced by the Old Chinese which is *trâuk.

SIMPLIFIED

wèn

mjuən^c

*məns

Ask

This character is a verb meaning to ask.

The components of this character have been modified to fit the changes in its phonetic development. It is the character for mouth in the character for door. In this case, the inner component provides a semantic reading, while the outer component provides a phonetic gloss.

In the context of the *Qianzi wen*, this character is bound to the one following it to make a word meaning to investigate or examine the principles.

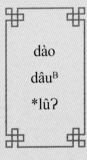

dào

dâu^B

*lû?

Way

At its most basic, this character represents a noun meaning road, way or path. However, this character is deeply enmeshed in the intellectual and philosophical traditions found throughout East Asia, with this term being generally translated into English as the Way or transliterated either using pinyin as Dao or Wade-Giles as Tao. This concept is complex and diverse and as stipulated in one of its earliest instantiations cannot be named or explained. The term is also applied to a large body of diverse ritual and religious traditions that have today come to be understood as Daoism.

Despite being so complex in meaning, its construction is rather straightforward, following basic phono-semantic principles. The left component is an abbreviated form of *chuò* 辵, meant to suggest motion or movement. The right component, *shōu* 首, means head, and although the Mandarin pronunciations do not match, it is reconstructed as *lhu? in Old Chinese.

In the context of the *Qianzi wen*, this character is bound to the one before it to make a word meaning to investigate or examine the principles.

chuí

źwie

*doi

Droop

This character means to droop or hang down. By extension it can mean to send down (orders, documents, etc.) or even to bequeath.

Despite its complex nature, this character is a pictogram, representing a very stylized picture of a willow tree, a tree noted for its hanging branches.

In the context of the *Qianzi wen*, this character is bound to the next one in a word that means to offer dutiful service (literally to bow one's head and clasp one's hands in respect).

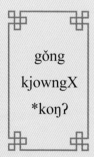

gǒng

kjowngX

*koŋ?

[A gesture of respect]

This character means to clasp one's hands in respect. This gesture involves one putting one's left hand over their right hand, which is held in a fist.

The character follows basic phono-semantic principles. The left component is the abbreviated form of the hand radical *shǒu* 手, serving as both the radical and semantic component. The left is a character pronounced as *gōng*, giving the phonetic gloss.

In the context of the *Qianzi wen*, this character is bound to the previous one in a word that means to offer dutiful service (literally to bow one's head and clasp one's hands in respect).

píng

bjaeng

*breŋ

Equal

This character means to be level or equal.

The meaning is suggested by the symmetry of the glyph. It is a pictogram of two items balanced at equal weight on a scale.

In the context of the *Qianzi wen*, this character is bound to the following one to make a word meaning to regulate or deliberate.

zhāng

tśjaŋ

*taŋ

Document

This character has a number of meanings, but originally referred to an official document or seal, which in the early period were not always distinct items. This has been occluded by its extended meanings such as a musical score, chapter of a document or section, which see more use in modern Mandarin.

Its construction has generated a common folk etymology, that it is the character for music, *yīn* 音, on top of the character for ten, *shí* 十, suggesting a compound meaning character. This explanation is somewhat dubious however, as neither component could suggest its sound. When looking at earlier examples of the glyph, however, it becomes clear that it is meant to be a pictogram of an official holding a document.

In the context of the *Qianzi wen*, this character is bound to the previous one to make a word meaning to regulate or deliberate.

Love

This character means love. In many premodern cultures, the concept of loyalty was more synonymous with love, and the virtues of love were often expressed in such terms in contrast to romantic love, which tends to be more emphasized in many modern cultures.

Ài is often explained as two hands holding a heart in the middle. The character for heart, a stylized pictogram, *xīn* 心, is present. However, this is most likely a folk etymology arising from stylization. Early glyphs of the character feature the character for loyalty *zhōng* 忠 with an additional component reflecting the link between the two concepts.

In the context of the *Qianzi wen*, this character is bound to the following one to make a word meaning to foster or nurture.

ài

Ɂâiᶜ

*Ɂə̂s

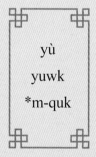

Raise

This character means to rear, raise or cultivate.

Although stylized with what looks like the moon radical, this may actually be an abbreviated form of *ròu* 肉, meaning meat. However, this is often argued to simply be a stylized version of earlier glyphs depicting a parent and a child, or even a mother giving birth.

In the context of the *Qianzi wen*, this character is bound to the previous one to make a word meaning to foster or nurture.

yù

yuwk

*m-quk

Li

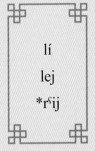

lí
lej
*r̥ij

This character is infrequent in modern Mandarin and is usually seen either as a surname or in compounds. In Classical Chinese its base meaning is multitudes or masses and it can also mean the colour black.

The character construction is a stylized combination of two characters which share a radical. Beyond this interesting fusion, it follows phono-semantic principles. The upper component provides the phonetic reading, *lì* 利, while the lower component is the character for millet, *shǔ* 黍. The character *hé* 禾, which refers to grain, is shared between them. This semantic value is relatively shallow to the overall meaning, however.

In the context of the *Qianzi wen*, this character is bound to the next one to create a noun meaning common people.

Head

shǒu
śjəuᴮ
*lhuʔ

This character means head. It can, by extension, refer to a leader or someone in charge.

The character is a very highly stylized pictogram of a person's head. However, the regularization of components has left it very similar to the word for 100, *bǎi* 百, resulting in some confusion.

In the context of the *Qianzi wen*, this character is bound to the one before it to create a noun meaning common people.

Vassal

This character means vassal or servant. In Classical Chinese, which operated a complex pronominal system, it can be used as a first person pronoun to express deference to the person one is speaking to.

It is a pictogram, and early examples, particularly in bronze inscriptions, show it to be highly eye-like. How this provides the meaning of vassal has produced a number of different explanations. One suggests that this is how one's eyes look when one's head is bowed.

In the context of the *Qianzi wen*, this character is bound to the next one to make a word that means to subdue or subjugate.

chén

źjen

*gin

Kneel

This character means to kneel or lie on the ground. By extension it can also mean to hide or be secretive.

This character is a compound meaning, as neither component could serve as a phonetic signifier in either modern Mandarin or Old Chinese. The character depicts both a human and a dog, *quǎn* 犬, with either the dog bowing to the human, or the character meant to insinuate a human kneeling like a dog.

In the context of the *Qianzi wen*, the character is bound to the previous one to make a word that means to subdue or subjugate.

fù

bjəuᶜ

*bəkh

róng

ńźjuŋ

*nuŋ

Weaponry

This character means weaponry, and by extension warfare, fighting and martialness. It is also a proper noun that is used for outsiders and others, particularly if they come from Central Asia. It may also have referred to a specific group of people who lived in Central Asia in very early texts.

Today it is identified as a combination of the word for ten, *shi* 十, and the word for halberd, *gē* 戈, providing semantic signifier. This 'ten' is a stylization of earlier ways of writing and may have been a picture of another weapon or perhaps a hand.

In the context of the *Qianzi wen*, this character is bound to the next character to create a word that refers generically to the peoples west of the area that is today called China.

qiāng

kʰjaŋ

*khaŋ

Qiang

This character is a proper noun. In early texts it was used to refer to peoples who inhabited areas in the western regions of China.

Today the character is argued to be the character *yáng* 羊 which refers to goats, with the character for person beneath it. However, earlier glyphs suggest it is actually a pictogram for some type of goat.

In the context of the *Qianzi wen*, this character is bound to the previous one to create a word that refers generically to the peoples west of the area that is today called China.

Far

This means to be far, distant.

This character has the movement radical, which serves as both a radical and a semantic component. Its right component is pronounced *xiá* and serves as the phonetic.

xiá

γa

*gâ

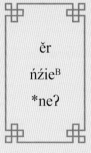

Near

This character means to be near or close

It follows the exact same construction as its antonym *xiá* 遐, far. This character has the movement radical, which serves as both a radical and a semantic component. Its right component is pronounced *ěr*, and serves as the phonetic.

SIMPLIFIED

ěr

ńźie^B

*ne?

SIMPLIFIED

yī

ʔjet

*ʔit

One

This character is the number one. This character is frequently used as a more formal iteration of the most basic character, *yī* 一, which is the conventional way to write the number one. However, owing to the ability to modify it, particularly into higher value numbers, this form is used to prevent any ambiguity or modification.

The construction of the character is not readily apparent from its current stylized form, as it reflects the fusion of its component characters. In this case, it is the character for pot, *hú* 壺, and the character for good fortune, *jí* 吉. The latter serves as the phonetic signifier, as its Old Chinese *kit is close to this character's Old Chinese pronunciation. How pot then serves as a semantic is rather unclear, and in this particular regard it most likely doesn't, and the character has been borrowed for its sound value only.

In the context of the *Qianzi wen*, this character is bound to the next one to mean entire or whole.

SIMPLIFIED

tǐ

tʰieiᴮ

*rhîʔ

Body

This character means body or structure.

The left component is the character *gǔ*, meaning bone, and provides the semantic value. The right component provides the phonetic value, though in Mandarin today this would be read as *lǐ*, while the Old Chinese value is reconstructed as *rîʔ.

In the context of the *Qianzi wen*, this character is bound to the previous one to mean entire or whole.

Lead

lǜ shuài

lwit srwit

*rut *s-rut

This character means to lead or command. When used in this capacity, it is meant to be read as *shuài* in modern Mandarin. When read as *lü4*, it means rate, ratio or portion.

    This character's construction is ambiguous. Early iterations suggest it is a pictogram, though of what is subject to debate. It has been suggested that they are birds caught in a net, but this may have come about due to its meaning to lead, rather than its true origin.

Guest

SIMPLIFIED

bīn

pjien

*pin

This character means guest or servant.

    The top component of the character is the 'roof' radical, which provides semantic significance. The bottom portion would be expected to provide the phonetic, but it is not a known character, and when looking at earlier forms of the glyph, they suggest it instead gives semantic meaning. The bottommost component is the character *běi* 貝, a pictogram of a cowrie shell which suggests money. The middle component has led to confusion among scholars, with some arguing it's a highly stylized form of *zhǐ* 止, meaning to stop, and others arguing it represents two people.

SIMPLIFIED

guī

kjwei

*kwəi

Return

This character means to return or go back; by extension it can mean to dwell on, to ponder as well as to pledge allegiance or swear loyalty.

The character is somewhat complex and subject to numerous folk etymologies. One suggests that it is a woman being married off and going to her new family. The right component is recognizable even early on as the character *zhǒu* 帚, which means, and is a pictogram for, a broom. This does not serve as a phonetic signifier, however, as its Old Chinese reconstruction, *t.pə?, is not close to this character's. The left components are stylized as recognizable components, and the lower component, *zhǐ* 止, which in earlier examples of the character actually looks more like 㞢, to go, may provide a semantic suggestion.

王

wáng

jwaŋᶜ

*waŋh

King

This character means king.

Owing to its importance, this character has been subject to a number of folk etymologies to explain its construction. One of the most popular is that the three horizontal lines indicate, from top to bottom: Heaven, Man, and Earth. The vertical line between them symbolizes the role of the king – to unite the three. While this provides insight into ideas of kingship and the moral and philosophical principles proposed by many scholars, it is not supported when one looks at examples of this glyph from the Oracle Bones or Bronze inscriptions.

The most likely origin is far more simple – it is a stylized pictogram of a king with the top line showing the crown, the middle the arms outstretched, and the bottom the bottom of a robe. These are not apparent as regularization has left them as horizontal lines, while the body has been reduced to a vertical line.

SIMPLIFIED

Tweet

This character means to call, tweet, squawk, sing or make any other noise associated with animals.

Both components contribute to a semantic understanding. The left is the character for mouth, while the right is the character for bird.

míng

mjwɐŋ

*mreŋ

SIMPLIFIED

Phoenix

This character refers to a mythical bird often translated into English as phoenix. Carrying significant cultural weight, depictions of this creature have varied over the centuries and its cultural identifications have equally shifted. However, it remains today an auspicious symbol employed by a variety of companies and individuals.

The outer portion of the character is also featured in the character *fēng* 風, for wind, with which it is often identified. This provides a phonetic gloss for the character. The inner part is a pictogram of a bird with a more elaborate comb than what is seen with *niǎo* 鳥.

fèng

bjuŋᶜ

*pəms

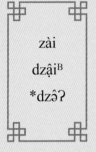

zài

dzậi[B]

*dzᵊ̂ʔ

At

This character means to be located in, to be at. By extension, it can sometimes means to exist. It is frequently employed in modern Mandarin as a coverb, indicating the location that an action takes place in.

Not readily apparent from how it has been stylized in modern orthographies, this character, despite appearing pictographic, follows the phonetic and semantic properties of the majority of characters. The component in the lower right is earth *tŭ* 土, which provides semantic value. The remainder of the character is made up of the character *cái* 才, which in Old Chinese would be *dzˤə.

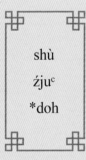

SIMPLIFIED

树

shù

źjuᶜ

*doh

Tree

This character means tree. As a verb it means to plant.

The component on the right is the character for tree, *mù* 木, and a synonym of this character. The right component suggests its phonetic value, which is evident in modern Mandarin, *shù*, and reinforced in Old Chinese with *doh. Additionally, early iterations of this character show it without the tree component. This may have been added as a hypercorrection, or the two characters may be etymologically related although suggesting different, but related concepts. The affixes added to *shù*'s 尌 Old Chinese pronunciation would suggest this.

bái

bɐk

*brâk

White

This character represents the colour white. By extension it can also mean related concepts such as purity and cleanliness. As a verb it means to confess or come clean.

It is a pictogram of the sun's light, with the line at the top emerging from the sun.

SIMPLIFIED

jū

kju

*ko

Foal

This character means a colt or foal.

The left component is the character for horse, indicating the semantic value as well as the radical. The right component indicates the phonetic value, as this is also *jù*.

Eat

This character represents the verb to eat. When read as *sì*, it means to feed. When used as a noun, this character stands for the word food.

The character's origins are ambiguous. It is most likely not built of a semantic and a phonetic component, as neither of the two components, *rén* 人 on the top and *liáng* 良 on the bottom are similar in sound in any form of Sinitic. A folk etymology suggests the two components' meanings as person and good indicate eating is when a person is good. Nonetheless, this is not borne out when looking at earlier iterations of the character, which would suggest it is a pictogram, though of what is not clear, and the modern components are the result of regularization of components.

shí sì

zyik ziH

*mə-lək

*s-m-lək-s

Field

This character means field or a large expanse of space.

The left component, the earth radical, provides some semantic meaning. Its right component is *yáng*, providing a shallow phonetic reading.

SIMPLIFIED

cháng

djaŋ

*d-laŋ

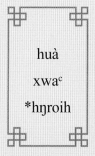

huà

xwa^c

*hŋroih

Change

This character means transform or change.

Both components have been regularized, with the person radical on the left and *bĭ* ヒ on the right, which obscures the character's origin. The latter refers to a small instrument, sometimes a spoon, other times a dagger. Neither gives a phonetic reading. Earlier forms of the character illustrate two shapes as mirror opposites of each other. These have sometimes been identified as people, but the inversion from the first to second shape is what provides the important semantic clue of change.

bèi

bjie^B

*bai?

Cover

As a verb, this character means to cover. As a noun it means blanket, quilt or some sort of covering. In modern Mandarin it is also a coverb that indicates the doer of an action in a passive sentence.

The left component of the character is a stylized *yī* 衣, which means clothing. The right side is today pronounced *pì*, but in Old Chinese it is reconstructed as *bai.

Grass

This character means grass.

It contains the grass radical as an upper component *cǎo* 艸, while the lower component is the character today pronounced as *zǎo*, but in Old Chinese it would have been something closer to *tsû?.

In the context of the *Qianzi wen*, it is bound to the next character to mean flora or plants in general.

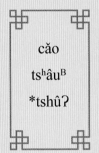

cǎo

tsʰâuᴮ

*tshû?

Tree

This character represents the word for tree.

The character is also employed as a radical by most dictionaries and features as a semantic component of many characters. Even despite its heavy stylization, it is still readily apparent as a pictogram of a tree.

In the context of the *Qianzi wen*, this character is bound to the one before it to mean flora or plants in general.

mù

muk

*môk

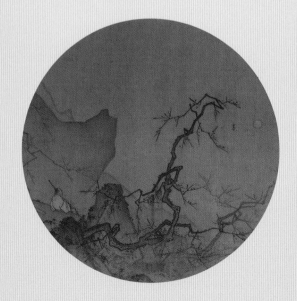

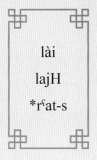

SIMPLIFIED

賴

lài

lajH

*rˤat-s

Rely

This character means to rely or to depend.

The left component of this character is the character *shū* while the right is the character *fù*. Neither would provide any phonetic value to the character in modern or old forms of Chinese. It is possible given these characters' meaning, to bind and to bear, that these both provide semantic significance.

及

jí

gjəp

*gəp

Reach

This character means to reach or come to. It is also employed as a conjunction to mean linear praxis, and a particle that connects two nouns, akin to 'and' in English.

The high level of stylization and regularization of this character has meant its origins are somewhat obscured. However, earlier iterations of this glyph show a hand and a person, which can be interpreted as someone leading someone else.

SIMPLIFIED

wàn

mjwɐnᶜ

*mans

10,000

This character represents the number 10,000, or by extrapolation a myriad, a lot or even all. In counting in many East Asian languages, the highest unit spoken before combining smaller units, what is referred to as the myriad, is 10,000. This differs from the 1,000 of English and many other Western languages. Hence to say one million in Mandarin, one would say *yī bái wàn* 一百萬, which would literally translate to one hundred ten thousands.

This character has the grass radical *cǎo* 艸 on the top and the character *yú* 禺 on the bottom. However, even when looking at older Chinese reconstructions, this bottom portion could not offer a phonetic reading. Early forms of this character show a pictogram. What it represents is somewhat unclear, but it is highly probable that the word is only used for its sound value, having been borrowed to represent 10,000.

In the context of the *Qianzi wen*, this character is bound to the following to mean everywhere.

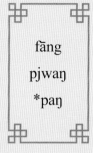

fāng

pjwaŋ

*paŋ

Square

This character means square or direction. By extrapolation, it can represent concepts such as place or side. It is also a time word in Classical Chinese that means right at this moment.

The construction of this character is very unclear. The earliest examples show a person above a horizontal line. It has been suggested that this represents a raft, a meaning put forward by commentary in some early texts and which would provide some relation to the more common meaning of square.

In the context of the *Qianzi wen*, this character is bound to the previous one to mean everywhere.

SIMPLIFIED

gài

kâi^c

*kâts

Cover

This character when used as a verb means to cover and as a noun means lid or cover. In Classical Chinese it can be used as an adverb meaning probably and as a particle. As a particle, its meaning is similar to the expressions 'on account of this' or 'considering that' in English.

The top portion is the grass radical *cǎo* 艸. The bottom portion is another character, *hé* 盍, which *gài* can actually stand in place for.

cǐ

tsʰieᴮ

*tsheʔ

This

This character stands for the demonstrative pronoun this. It can also occasionally be used as a third person pronoun in Classical Chinese. It has been displaced as a standard demonstrative pronoun in modern Mandarin by *zhè* 這, though it is still used in some formal applications and various compounds and idioms.

Though stylized with a *zhǐ* 止 on the left and a *bǐ* 匕 on the right, earlier iterations had a *zhǐ* and a *rén* 人, thus suggesting that this iteration is merely the result of stylization.

shēn

śjen

*lhinʔ

Body

This character means body or self.

The character is a pictogram of a person's body. It has become highly stylized in modern orthography.

fǎ

pjwɐt

*pat

Hair

This character means hair, generally in reference to the hair on a human's head.

The top component of the character is *biāo* 髟, a somewhat obscure word that means hair or hairy, thus suggesting the semantic component. The bottom portion is pronounced *fà* 发 in its own right, and today is used as the *jiantizi* for this character.

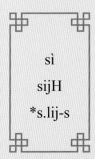

sì

sijH

*s.lij-s

Four

This character represents the number four. In modern East Asia, the number four is considered an 'unlucky' number. The reason is that it is a homophone of the word for death, *sǐ* 死.

Most characters for numbers derive from the image formed from counting rods, but in the number four's case, this would yield the glyph 亖. The earliest examples of this character are a pictogram, but of what is not entirely clear. Some believe it represents an elephant's head, suggesting the glyph was borrowed owing to phonetic similarity to the word for four.

In the context of the *Qianzi wen*, this character is bound to the next one to create a word which means the four elements – fire, wind, water and earth.

Big

This character represents the verb to be big, large, great.

It is a pictogram of a person standing with their arms and legs spread out.

In the context of the *Qianzi wen*, this character is bound to the previous one to create a word which means the four elements – fire, wind, water and earth.

dà

dâi^c

*dâs

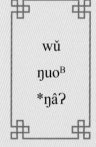

Five

This character represents the number five.

This character is a pictogram of the counting rods used to display numbers. It has become stylized through the character's regularization, as the earliest iterations would have shown two horizontal lines with two diagonal lines, resembling a letter X, between them.

In the context of the *Qianzi wen*, this character is bound to the next character to create a word which means the five phases – fire, wood, water, earth and metal. This concept, which was widely used at the beginning of the first millennium, correlates many natural phenomena with one of these 'phases', which exist in a cycle of mutual creation and destruction.

wǔ

ŋuo^B

*ŋâʔ

cháng
źjaŋ
*daŋ

Often

This character represents one of the common false friends between Classical Chinese and modern Mandarin. In Classical Chinese this is a time word meaning always. It can also be a verb meaning to be constant, or a noun meaning constancy. In modern Mandarin it is a time word meaning often.

Like the character *cháng* 裳, this character shares the upper *shàng* 尚 portion that provides a phonetic gloss for this character. The bottom component is *jīn* 巾, which provides the semantic meaning. *Jīn* itself means a piece of cloth, and how this relates to its use as a time word is unclear, suggesting it may be a phonetic borrowing.

In the context of the *Qianzi wen*, this character is bound to the next one to create a word which means the five phases – fire, wood, water, earth and metal. This concept, which was widely used at the beginning of the first millennium, correlates many natural phenomena with one of these 'phases', which exist in a cycle of mutual creation and destruction.

gōng
kjowng
*koŋ

To be respectful

This character represents the verb to be respectful.

The upper component of the character, pronounced *gōng* 共, provides the phonetic value, and the lower component, an abbreviated heart radical *xīn* 心, provides the semantic value.

In the context of the *Qianzi wen*, this character is bound to the next one to be a verb meaning to flatter, praise or compliment.

惟

Only

This character represents the adverb only. Further, it was a linking word in pre-classical Chinese.

wéi

ywij

*ɢʷij

Given the number of variant forms of this character which switch out the heart radical, *xīn* 心, for other components, concern for any semantic value does not seem to be an issue for this character, and it most likely was 'borrowed' due to its sound to be used for many different words.

In the context of the *Qianzi wen*, this character is bound to the one before it to make a verb meaning to flatter, praise or compliment.

鞠

Bring up

This character means to rear or bring up.

jú

kjuk

*kuk

The left component of the character is *gé* 革, which is employed as the radical, and means leather or hide, a shallow semantic value which may suggest either other meanings or phonetic borrowing. The right component provides the phonetic reading as it is read as *jū*.

In the context of the *Qianzi wen*, this character is bound to the next one to make a word that means to rear or nurture.

SIMPLIFIED

yǎng

jiaŋ^c

*jaŋh

Bring up

This character means to raise, bring up or support.

It follows phono-semantic principles, though the two component characters have been adjusted slightly to accommodate each other. The top component is *yáng* 羊, providing the phonetic gloss. The bottom component *shì* 食, to eat, provides the semantic gloss.

In the context of the *Qianzi wen*, this character is bound to the previous one to make a word that means to rear or nurture.

SIMPLIFIED

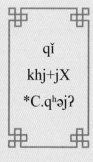

qǐ

khj+jX

*C.qʰəjʔ

[Rhetorical question]

This character represents a rhetorical question particle. It would be equivalent in English to asking 'How can it…?'

The current composition of the character would suggest that it has the character for mountain, *shān* 山, above the character for bean, *dǒu* 豆. Neither provide a phonetic gloss either in modern or older forms of the language, and they are the result of regularization of components. The earliest examples of this character appear to be pictographic, but of what is subject to debate.

Dare

This character means to dare.

The right component is not a character in its own right but is clearly the regularization of a component which in earlier iterations represented a hand. The left component is more confusing as it is somewhat diverse, though the modern glyph features what would appear to be *ěr* 耳, an ear.

gǎn
kâm[B]
***kâm?**

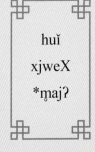

Destroy

This character means to damage or destroy.

The right component is *shū* 殳, the lower left component is *tǔ* 土, and the upper component resembles the character *jiù* 臼, which represents a mortar. None of these components offers a reliable phonetic gloss for the character, which would suggest it is not a phono-semantic compound. This may be the result of regularization of units, and earlier units may suggest a hand breaking an object.

In the context of the *Qianzi wen*, this character is bound to the next character to create a word that means to damage or harm.

huǐ
xjweX
***m̥aj?**

SIMPLIFIED

shāng

śjaŋ

*lhaŋ

Harm

This character means to harm, damage or hurt.

The left component is apparent as the abbreviated form of the character for person. The right component provides the phonetic gloss as it is pronounced as *shāng* on its own.

In the context of the *Qianzi wen*, this character is bound to the previous character to create a word that means to damage or harm.

Woman

This character means female, woman or girl.

The character is one of the most basic and is a radical in most dictionaries, often being a component of other characters. Given its fundamental nature, it is likely a pictogram. A common folk etymology suggests that it is a person who is pregnant, but earlier forms of the glyphs indicate a figure seated with their arms crossed.

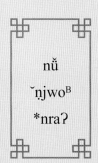

nǔ

ˇnjwoᴮ

*nraʔ

Admire

This character is a verb meaning to admire or yearn for.

The bottom portion is a stylized heart *xīn* 心, providing semantic significance. The top portion is mò 莫, which provides the phonetic.

mù

muoᶜ

*mâkh

Loyal

This character means to be loyal or faithful to.

The character depicts the cracking of a cowrie shell. This was an act of divination similar to the method used to create the oracle bones, which involved heating oxen scapulae and turtle plastron. Though this does not have any semantic value for the character's modern meaning, it may have an archaic meaning of to divine, and hence may be a very early phonetic borrowing.

In the context of the *Qianzi wen*, the character is bound to the next one to make a word meaning chastity. This highlights the prescriptive gendered norms of the era. The text was written by men and intended to educate only men, as women were prohibited from sitting the civil-service exam and so would only be educated if their families wished it.

SIMPLIFIED

zhēn

ʈjäŋ

*treŋ

SIMPLIFIED

jié

kiet

*kêt

Clean

This character means to be clean or to clean.

The lower component of the character is the cloth radical mì 糸. The upper right component is *dāo* 刀, the character for blade, while the upper left is a component assigned the pronunciation of *fēng* 丰. None of these provide any meaningful phonetic value, and cloth can provide only a very shallow semantic suggestion. This is the result of the stylization of the components, and earlier iterations suggest it may have pictographic qualities of a person (the upper right component) hanging cloth (the lower component) on a rail (the upper left component). This character is now frequently written with the addition of the water radical on the left, 潔, to align it to phono-semantic principles.

In the context of the *Qianzi wen*, the character is bound to the previous one to make a word meaning chastity. This highlights the prescriptive gendered norms of the era. The text was written by men and intended to educate only men, as women were prohibited from sitting the civil-service exam and so would only be educated if their families wished it.

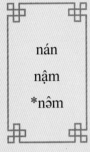

nán

nậm

*nə̂m

Man

This character means male, man or boy.

This character is a traditional compound meaning character with a field, *tián* 田, at the top and the character, *lì* 力, at the bottom, a noun which means power. The standard folk etymology suggests that it represents either exerting oneself in the fields or the responsibilities of a man – to be powerful and have land. These illustrate the gender norms of the society that employed them, but the earliest iteration of the glyph actually have slightly different components, though do still largely fit with this interpretation. The bottom component is a product of stylization, with earlier iterations depicting either a hand or a pitchfork next to a field.

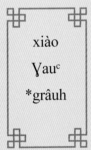

xiào

ɣauᶜ

*grâuh

Imitate

This character means to imitate or follow the example of. It also means to be effective or take an effect.

The left component is the character *jiāo* 交, which provides the phonetic value for the character. The right component is *pū* 攵, which features in many characters, but lacks any meaning on its own. With the earlier iterations of this character, it would appear as a hand with a tool, which provides a shallow semantic gloss.

cái

dzoj

*dzˤə

Skilled

This character means to be skilled or talented as a verb. It is also used in modern Mandarin as a modal adverb; in practice it means that the action of the sentence is unexpected or a change, at least from the perspective of the speaker.

The character, as its highly simplistic form suggests, is a pictogram. It is often suggested that this is a young plant. It has clearly been borrowed for its phonetic value with regard to the words it is used as today.

In the context of the *Qianzi wen*, it is bound to the following character to mean the talented and worthy.

liáng

ljang

*raŋ

Good

This character means to be good.

The construction of the character is unclear. The earliest examples are ambiguous as to what they represent and we cannot say with any degree of certainty how it was formed.

In the context of the *Qianzi wen*, it is bound to the previous character to mean the talented and worthy.

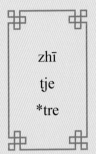

zhī

tje

*tre

Know

This character means to know.

The left component is the character *shǐ* 矢, which means an arrow; the right component is the character for mouth, *kǒu* 口. It has generally been argued that this is an example of a 'compound meaning character', although it conforms more to phono-semantic principles.

SIMPLIFIED

guò

kuâᶜ

*kôih

To cross

This character represents a number of words. As a verb it can mean to cross, pass over or surpass. It also can mean to err or do wrong. As a noun it means error, fault or wrong. In modern Mandarin it is also a particle that when placed behind a verb indicates experience, as in 'having done'.

The character conforms to phono-semantic principles. The left component is *chuò* 辵, which often suggests movement. The right component is *guō* 咼, which provides the phonetic gloss. Its multiple meanings demonstrate the use of the same glyph for different words that are homophones.

bì

pjiet

*pit

To be certain

This character means to be certain, sure or necessary.

In appearance, the modern glyph resembles the character for heart *xīn* ⼼ with a stroke over it. This has given rise to a folk etymology that what one 'must' do is 'marked' by one's 'heart', which provides a poetic, if shallow, explanation. Nonetheless, the character has been regularized with these more standard components, and its earlier glyph does not suggest these components. In its original form, it seems to show the counting rods for the number eight and what looks like a cudgel or rod.

gǎi

kậiᶜ

*kə?

Change

This character represents a verb meaning to change, transform or alter.

As with many other examples seen, the origin of this character is ambiguous. Unlike other cases where the regularization of components has led to some degree of obscurity, the glyph of this character in use today is very much akin to its earlier iterations. The left component is the character *jǐ* 己 and the right component is the character *pū* 攴. How these suggest the meaning of change is unclear. It is likely it represents a phonetic borrowing.

dé

tək

*tə̂k

Get

This character means to get or obtain. As in English, it can be used metaphorically to mean understand. In modern Mandarin, when read as *děi*, it means to be able to. As a homophone for the word for virtue, represented by the character *dé* 德, and having a long philosophical pedigree, it is also seen in place of that character as well.

The left component is an abbreviated form of the character *xíng* 行. The right components have been stylized to resemble the character for sun, a horizontal line and the character for inch, *cún* 寸. However, these are products of regularization, and earlier iterations showed a hand below a cowrie shell – something more suggestive of its semantic meaning.

néng

nəŋ

*nə̂

Can

This character represents the verb to be able to, can. It can also be a noun meaning ability.

The character is commonly understood as a pictogram, despite many of its components having been regularized to standard components. The earliest iterations show a pictogram of a bear, which is now written 熊 and pronounced as *xiōng*. However, these two characters do not share a similar pronunciation in modern Mandarin or Old Chinese.

mò

mâk

*mâk

In no case

This character represents a negator seen frequently in Classical Chinese and seen in compounds in modern Mandarin. All forms of Chinese have a number of different adverbs that negate a sentence in different ways. These are most diverse in Classical Chinese and have been reduced in number in most modern varieties such as Mandarin. In Classical Chinese, this means that 'in no case' does the verbal action take place. This character is also used at times for the time word 'dawn' which is now usually written as 暮 and read *mù*. Although pronounced differently today, their exchange suggests that they would have been homophonous in the past.

The composition of the modern glyph has the grass radical at the top, what appears to be a sun in the middle and the character for big, *dà* 大, at the bottom. These are products of the regularization of components with earlier iterations showing grass on both the top and the bottom and the glyph for the sun in the centre. Either the sense of 'dawn' was an earlier meaning and it has just been borrowed for phonetic value, or they are both phonetic borrowings.

Forget

This character refers to the verb to forget or neglect.

The character has the heart character at the bottom, often used for words relating to emotions and the mind. The top portion is a character read as *wáng* 亡, and so clearly provides the phonetic reading.

wàng

mjwaŋ

*maŋ

Not

This character represents a pre-classical negator, equivalent to *bù* 不 in Classical Chinese and modern varieties of Chinese. Although knowledge of pre-classical Chinese is not as detailed as Classical Chinese, texts written in it would form the basis for the civil service exam and so it was important for scholars to be aware of certain aspects of it. Additionally, these archaisms would find continued use in later writings and indeed still occur in some modern compounds.

The character is a fusion of the 'net' component and the character *wáng* 亡. It is most likely a phonetic borrowing owing to the ambiguity of its semantic suggestions.

wǎng

mjwaŋ^B

*maŋ?

SIMPLIFIED

tán

dâm

*lâm

Talk

This character means to talk or chat.

The left component, the water radical, *yán* 言, suggests its semantic value. The right component is today read as *yán* though in Old Chinese the sounds were more homophonous with it being closer to *lam.

bǐ

pje^B

*pai?

That

This character is a demonstrative pronoun equivalent to the English that. It can also be used as a third person pronoun in Classical Chinese and has taken on that role regularly in Japanese. Although displaced by the word *nà* 那 in modern Mandarin, it is still seen in formal applications and in compounds.

The left component of the character is a stylized *xíng* 行 which means to walk or go. The right side is today pronounced *pì*, but in Old Chinese it is reconstructed as *bai.

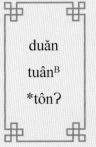

duǎn

tuân[B]

*tôn?

Short

This character means to be short.

The right component is *shǐ*, meaning arrow and the left component is *dǒu* 豆, meaning bean. How these two provide either a semantic or phonetic gloss is unclear and suggests that this may be a phonetic borrowing.

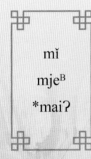

mǐ

mje[B]

*mai?

Not

This character represents a pre-classical negator similar to *wáng* 罔 (see page 137). What difference there is between the two is not entirely clear, and it now exists only as a preserved archaism.

The upper component is the character *mā* 麻, which means hemp, but is used here for its phonetic value, while the lower component is *fēi*, another negator, though only for nominal sentences, a type of sentence lacking verbs in Classical Chinese. It originates as a combination of *bù* 不 and *wéi* 惟 in pre-classical Chinese.

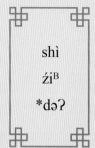

shì

źi^B

*də?

Depend

This character represents the verb to rely or depend on.

This character follows phono-semantic principles. The left component is the abbreviated heart radical, suggesting something to do with emotions or the mind, and the right is the character *sì* 寺, which means temple, but here provides a phonetic gloss.

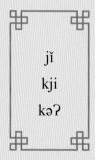

jǐ

kji

kə?

Self

This character represents the reflexive pronoun, and is thus equivalent to myself, yourself, oneself, etc. in English.

As with many of the other most basic glyphs, this is a pictogram, but it is highly impressionistic even in earlier iterations, perhaps representing a piece of string. It is most likely a phonetic borrowing. Its simplicity also leads it to be confused with two very similar looking characters *yǐ* 已 and *sì* 巳, particularly when written by hand, though their use is very different and so can usually be discerned through context.

SIMPLIFIED

cháng zhǎng

ḍjaŋ tjaŋᴮ

*draŋ *traŋ?

Long

When read as *cháng* this character means to be long. When read as *zhǎng* the character means to be older or more senior.

The character is a pictogram of a person with long hair, which earlier iterations do also seem to bear similarity to, although they tend to be more complex than the current glyph.

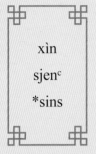

xìn

sjen^c

*sins

Trustworthy

This character is a verb meaning to be trustworthy. It can also mean to believe or have faith in. As a noun it means sincerity or faith. In modern Mandarin it is also used to refer to a letter one would write to a person.

The character has the character for speech on the right, *yán* 言, and the character for person, *rén* 人, on the left. This suggests a semantic value reflecting the idiom 'one's word is one's bond'. Neither could provide a phonetic gloss in modern or older forms of Chinese.

shì

ṣi^c

*srəh

Send

This character refers to a verb meaning either to send, dispatch or to cause, make. It can also be a noun meaning messenger or envoy. When used as a sentence particle it means if or when.

The left component is the person radical *rén* 人, while the right component is the character *lǐ* 吏, meaning official or clerk. As neither provides any reliable phonetic component, they are probably meant to be understood semantically. Its large number of meanings also suggest a high level of phonetic borrowing amongst homophones.

可

kě

kʰâᴮ

*khâi?

Acceptable

This character means to be acceptable, possible. It is often seen as an auxiliary verb meaning to be able to.

The outer portion of the character is a stylization of the components in earlier iterations, sometimes suggested to be a person. The character includes the character for mouth, *kŏu*, and this may suggest a semantic reading, indicating a person speaking, supported by the character *hè* 呵, which means to shout. This character has shifted to its current meanings owing to phonetic borrowing.

覆

SIMPLIFIED

复

fù

pʰjuk

*phuk

Invert

This character means either to invert or turn over, and by extension can mean reply, or to cover.

The upper portion of the character is a radical component that is not a character in its own right, but is labelled as *yà* and is attributed the semantic meaning of to cover. The bottom component, read as *fù* 復, provides the phonetic value, and is sometimes seen in place of the one above, suggesting the radical was added to disambiguate and may reflect the Old Chinese system of affixes.

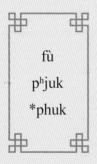

qì

khijH

*kʰrət-s

Vessel

This character means vessel, implement or ware.

The character appears composed of four mouths with a *dà* 大 or *quǎn* 犬 depending on the style between them. This is surprisingly close to earlier iterations. It is meant to illustrate a dog guarding vessels, as dogs were traditionally used to protect storehouses.

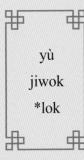

yù

jiwok

*lok

Want

This character is a verb meaning to want or desire. It is also used as an auxiliary verb that indicates potentiality, equivalent to 'going to' in English. It has generally been displaced in modern Mandarin by other words, but is still seen in idioms and compounds.

The left component is the character *gǔ* 谷, meaning valley, but likely here for its phonetic value, the Old Chinese reconstruction also being *lok. The right component is the character *qiàn*, which means to lack, and may offer the semantic value.

SIMPLIFIED

难

nàn nán

nânᶜ nân

*nâns *nân

Difficult

When read as *nán*, this character means to be difficult, hard. When read as *nàn*, this character means a calamity or disaster. This tone difference is most likely a vestige of Old Chinese's system of affixes.

The right component is the character *zhuī* 隹, which is meant to provide the semantic value, though as a pictogram of a bird this seems tenuous at best. The left component is found in a variety of characters with similar pronunciations – *hàn* 漢, *tàn* 歎 – but is not a character in its own right nor has it been made into a radical, despite providing phonetic value to a number of characters.

liàng

ljaŋᶜ

*raŋh

Measure

This character means to measure and by extension appraise.

The character today has the character for dawn, *dàn* 旦, above the character for village, *lǐ* 里. Neither would provide a suitable phonetic gloss for this character in any form of Chinese. Earlier iterations suggest it is a pictogram, showing an item on a scale.

mò

mək

*mək

Ink

This character refers to the noun ink, and by extension can mean black or dark. It is also a surname shared by the culture hero named Mo Di but more often referred to as Mozi, one of the many notable thinkers from the Warring States period. The text associated with him, also labelled the *Mozi*, is often cited in later philosophical debate and is still discussed and analyzed today.

The character has the character for black, *hēi* 黑, above the character for earth. Where both characters can provide semantic values, the top character in Old Chinese is reconstructed as *hmək. This similarity not only suggests a phonetic signifier, but indeed its similarity may indicate that one is modified from the other. The earth component may have been added to mark the alteration.

bēi

pij

*prəi

Sad

This character means to be sad or sorrowful.

The character contains the heart component below the character *fēi*, which though a rhyme in modern Mandarin would be in *pəj.

SIMPLIFIED

Silk

This character means silk.

It is made up of the cloth radical, *mì* 糸, reduplicated and thus provides a clear, albeit stylized pictogram.

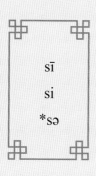

sī
si
*sə

Dye

This character means to dye or to be dyed, and by extension to be polluted or tainted.

The upper left component is the abbreviated form for water, *shuǐ* 水, which would also provide semantic meaning, while the remaining part of the character shows a nine, *jiǔ* 九, over a tree, *mù* 木. These components would not provide meaningful phonetic values in modern or old varieties of Chinese. Some clue may be gleamed in earlier iterations of the glyph, where the upper right component has similarities to other glyphs for hand, suggesting this may be the result of regularization of components.

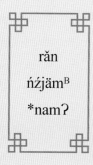

rǎn
ńʑjämᴮ
*nam?

SIMPLIFIED

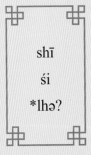

shī

śi

*lhə?

Poetry

This character reflects a noun that today means poetry in general. It also means a specific mode of poetry, which is the mode of poetry used to write the *Qianzi wen*. It can also be used as a metonym for a text called the *Shijing*, sometimes called the *Odes* or *Book of Songs* in English. Composed of 300 poems purportedly from the first millennium BCE, this text made up one of the basic texts expected to be memorized by candidates for the Civil Service exam.

The left component is the character for speech. The right component provides the phonetic value being pronounced *sì* on its own.

SIMPLIFIED

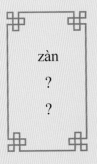

zàn

?

?

Praise

This character means to praise.

It has the character for speech as its left component, while the right component provides the phonetic gloss, being pronounced as *zàn* in modern Mandarin.

gāo

kâu

*kâu?

Lamb

This character means lamb.

The character's top portion is a truncated iteration of the character for goat, *yáng* 羊. The bottom portion is the abbreviated form of fire, *huǒ* 火. The character is a compound meaning character suggesting the type of goat one cooks.

In the context of the *Qianzi wen*, this character is bound to the next one to mean not only lamb, but also the title of one of the poems found in the *Shijing*.

羊

yáng

jiaŋ

*jaŋ

Goat

This character features as a component in many other characters. It represents a noun meaning a goat or sheep.

It is a pictogram of the head of a goat with the lines indicating its silhouette.

In the context of the *Qianzi wen*, this character is bound to the prior one to mean not only lamb, but also the title of one of the poems found in the *Shijing*.

jǐng

kjɐŋ^B

*kraŋʔ

View

This character means view or scenery. It can also mean situation, by extension.

The upper component of the character is the character for sun. The lower component is the character *jīng* 京, which provides the phonetic value.

In the context of the *Qianzi wen*, this character is bound to the next one to make a word meaning lofty virtue.

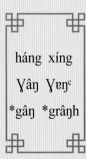

háng xíng

ɣâŋ ɣɐŋ^c

*gâŋ *grâŋh

Behave

When read as *xíng*, this character means to walk, though it is rarely used that way in modern Mandarin. It also means to behave, as well as the nominal meaning of behaviour. When read as *hàng* it is a noun meaning line. Found in many words in modern Mandarin, it can also be used to indicate acceptance or agreement of a proposed course of action.

The character is a highly stylized pictogram of the intersection of two roads.

In the context of the *Qianzi wen*, this character is bound to the previous one to make a word meaning lofty virtue.

wéi

ywij

*ɢʷij

Tie up

This character means to tie up, and by extension preserve or maintain.

The left component is the cloth radical, which clearly aligns with the semantic meaning of tying up. The right is the character *zhuī*, which would have been pronounced as *tur. This does not fit well with the reconstructed Old Chinese, however, suggesting that this may not be a phonetic signifier, but rather may provide semantic value – cloth used to tie up a bird.

SIMPLIFIED

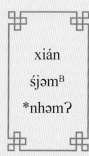

xián

śjəmᴮ

*nhəmʔ

Worthy

This character represents a verb meaning to be worthy. It can also be used nominally to mean worthies.

Its lower component is the character *běi* 貝, a cowrie shell, which features in many characters to suggest money. The upper left component is the character *chén* 臣, meaning vassal or subject. The upper right component is the character *yòu* 又, however this is the result of regularization as the earlier iterations showed a hand. None of these characters could provide a useful phonetic gloss for the character either in modern or older forms of the language, and so this may suggest some semantic interpretation. As cowrie shells could also serve as signs of rank, their 'award' to a deserving vassal may signify their worth.

SIMPLIFIED

kè

kʰək

*khə̂k

Conquer

This character means to overcome, conquer or subdue.

This character is often written without the right component, an abbreviated form of *dāo* 刀, so it often appears as just 克. The earliest iterations appear to be pictograms, perhaps of a shoulder. The addition of the blade radical may be a hypercorrection is an attempt to provide some clearer semantic value.

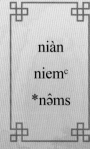

niàn

niemᶜ

*nə̂ms

Think

This character as a verb means to think, miss, or reminisce. As a noun it means thought or idea. In Buddhist contexts, it can mean to dwell upon in meditation.

The character contains the heart character at the bottom, providing semantic value. The component at the top should provide the phonetic reading. While the modern Mandarin *jīn* does not provide a suitable phonetic component, the Old Chinese *kəm does.

zuò

tsâk

tsâk

Write

This character represents a number of words. Its basic meaning is as a verb, to arise; however, it is more frequently used in derived meanings such as to produce or create. Given the strong relationship between writing and Literati Culture, it also can be derived to mean to write and used as a noun to mean writings. It can also mean to pretend. The character is also often used in place of the homophone *zuò* 做, which means to do.

Belying its simplicity, the character follows phono-semantic principles with the left component being the character for person. The right component is today pronounced *zhà,* which does not provide a useful phonetic gloss in modern Mandarin, but the Old Chinese would have been closer as *dzˤrak-s.

SIMPLIFIED

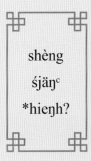

shèng

śjäŋᶜ

*hieŋh?

Sage

This character means sage. It is also used to translate the concept of saint in the Bible.

This character is subject to a number of folk etymologies. One common one is that it is meant to illustrate a 'king', from the *wáng* 王 below, who listens with his 'ears' *ěr* 耳 to the words spoken from the mouths, *kǒu* 口, of others. Another explanation suggests it is the king who speaks with his mouth and others who listen listens. In both cases, this suggests a sage is a person who heeds advice. Although this may be a noble explanation of what a sage is, in fact the ear component serves as the radical and semantic component while the character *chěng* 呈 serves as the phonetic component.

Further Reading

Boltz, William G. *The origin and early development of the Chinese writing system*. New Haven: American Oriental Society (1994).

Keightley, David. *Sources of Shang history: the oracle-bone inscriptions of bronze-age China*. Berkeley: University of California Press (1978).

Norman, Jerry. *Chinese*. Cambridge: Cambridge University Press (1988).

Qiu Xigui. *Chinese writing*. Gilbert L. Mattos; Jerry Norman (trs). Berkeley: Society for the Study of Early China and The Institute of East Asian Studies, University of California (2000).

Zhou Youguang. *The Historical Evolution of Chinese Languages and Scripts*. Zhang Liqing (trs.). Columbus: National East Asian Languages Resource Center, Ohio State University (2003).

Baxter, William H. and Sagart, Laurent. *Old Chinese: A New Reconstruction*, Oxford University Press (2014).

Chou, H. *Ch'ien tzu wen the thousand character classic: a Chinese primer*. New York: F. Ungar Pub. Co (1963).

Denecke, Wiebke; Li, Wai-yee; Tian, Xiaofei (eds.). *The Oxford Handbook of Classical Chinese Literature (1000 BCE-900 CE)*. New York, NY: Oxford University Press (2017).

Owen, Stephen (ed.). *The Cambridge History of Chinese Literature, vol. 1: To 1375*. Cambridge: Cambridge University Press (2010).

Schuessler, Axel. *ABC Etymological Dictionary of Old Chinese*. Honolulu: University of Hawai'i Press (2007).

Wilkinson, Endymion. *Chinese History: A New Manual*. Cambridge, MA: Harvard University Asia Center (2012).

Yang, Lihui and An Deming. *Handbook of Chinese Mythology*. Oxford: Oxford University Press (2008).

Index of Characters

10,000: wàn 萬116

A

acceptable: kě 可143
accomplish: chéng 成38
activate: zhāng 張30
admire: mù 慕128
afternoon: zè 昃27
agreement: hang 150
allow: ràng 讓83
alter see change
always: cháng 常123
and: jí 115
appear: zhāng 張30
   see also zhì 致45
appraise: liàng 量145
arise: zuò 作153
army: shī 70
arrive: zhì 致45
ask: wèn 問96
at: zài 在110
attack: fá 伐89
august: huáng 皇76
autumn: qiū 秋33

B

bamboo pipes: lǚ 呂39
be: wèi or wéi 為47
beautiful: lì 麗50
become: chéng 成38
   see also wèi or wéi 為47
begin see start
behave: xìng 行150
believe: xìn 信142
bequeath: chuí 垂97

big: dà 大122
   see also hóng 洪25
bird: niǎo 鳥73
birth: sheng 生49
bland: dàn 淡66
black: : lí 黎100 see also mò 墨146
blanket: bèi 被113
body: tǐ 體104 see also shēn 身118
boy: nán 男130
bring up: jú 鞠124
   see also yǎng 養125
brown: huáng 黃23

C

calamity see disaster
call: chēng 稱57
can: néng 能134
   see also dé 得134 and kě 143
capital: guó 國84
cause: shì 使142
certain: bì 必133
change: huà 化113
   see also gǎi 改133
character: zì 字79
chat see talk
clean: jié 絜129 see also bái 白111
close see near
clothing: yì or yī 衣81
   see also fú 80 and cháng 裳81
clouds: yún 雲44
cold: hán 寒31
colt see foal
command see lead
come: lái 來31
complete: chéng 成38

155

T
tainted: rǎn 染147
talk: tán 談138
Tang (dynasty): tang 唐87
Tao *see* way
talented *see* skilled
teacher: shī 師70
that: bǐ 彼138
then: nǎi 乃80
thin: dàn 淡66
think: niàn 念152
this: cǐ 此118
tie up: wéi 維151
time: zhòu 宙24
tone: diào 調41
transfer: diào 調41
transform *see* change
treasure: zhēn 珍59
tree: shù 樹110 *see also* mù 木114
trustworthy: xìn 信142
tune: diào 調41
tweet: míng 鳴109

U
unknown: xuán 玄23

V
vassal: chén 臣101
vessel: qì 器144
view: jǐng 景150

W
walk: xìng 150
want: yù 欲144
ware *see* vessel
warfare: róng 戎102
warm: shǔ 暑32
water: shuǐ 水52
way: dào 道96
weaponry: róng 戎102
wear: fú 服80
weight: zhòng 重61
when: shì 142
white: bái 白111
wilderness: huāng 荒25
winter: dōng 冬34
  see also hán 寒31
woman: nǚ 女127
worthy: xián 賢151
writing: wén 文79
  see also zuò 作153

Y
yang: yáng 陽42
year: suì 歲38
yearn *see* admire
yellow: huáng 黃23
Yellow River: hé 河66
yield: ràng 讓83
yin: yīn 殷92

Z
Zhou (dynasty): zhōu 周90